A Knave Among Knights in their Spitfires

Chevalier Jerry Billing M.I.D., C.D., M.G.C.

Upper Canada Press
Ontario, Canada - Nashville, Tennessee

Copyright © 2011 Jerry Billing

All rights reserved. No part of this book may be transmitted in any form by any means electronic, mechanical or otherwise using devices now existing or yet to be invented without prior written permission from the publisher and copyright holder.

****
PLEASE NOTE

This 2011 edition of Jerry Billing's book is as far as possible an exact reproduction of a 1995 printing. In order to expedite its printing, Upper Canada Press has not edited or altered it to any significant extent, and can assume no responsibility for the accuracy of its contents.
****

Upper Canada Press

an imprint of

American History Press

Franklin, Tennessee

(888) 521-1789

Visit us on the Internet at:

www.Americanhistorypress.com

ISBN 13: 978-0-9830827-3-6

Library of Congress Control Number: 2011930848

Printed in the United States of America on acid-free paper.

This book meets all ANSI standards for archival quality.

Photo by Spike Bell

JERRY BILLING MID, CD, MGC.
A Knave among Knights
in their Spitfires

DEDICATION

This book is dedicated to my beautiful (Danish) wife - who constantly urges me to fly, and to continue flying until I cannot get into an aircraft.

"A Real Viking" KAREN.

Love
Jerry

Jerry Billings stands beside a crashed Spitfire on display in France, 1996

TABLE OF CONTENTS

Introduction	1
Acknowledgements	5
Forward	6
Comment	7
Prologue	8
Chapter 1 Pre-War Days and Enlistment	11
Chapter 2 Training Days in Canada	16
Chapter 3 Overseas Operational Training	18
Chapter 4 #19 Squadron, 1942	24
Chapter 5 Malta Blitz, ('4243')	29
Chapter 6 Spitfire O.T.U. Instructor and One Month's Leave in Canada	64
Chapter 7 Shot Down, Escape and Evasion	80
Chapter 8 Repatriation and Discharge - Canada 1944-1947	95
Chapter 9 Re-Enlistment 1948 R.C.A.F.	101
Chapter 10 Jet Tactics and Weapons Unit, 129 Test and Ferry Unit	110
Chapter 11 Test Pilot DeHavilland Canada, Vietnam 1965-1966	113
Chapter 12 Spitfires	119
Chapter 13 Fifty Years Later	130
Chapter 14 My Airstrip	136
In Memory Of	140
Lest We Forget	142
Comments	143
Final Words	148

Jerry's decoration awarded by France. "The Knight of the Order of Merit" (Chevalier dans l'Ordre National du Mérite).

Introduction

by Cliff Robertson

KNIGHTS OF BATTLE

Cliff Robertson, Academy-Award winning actor, pilot, aircraft enthusiast and owner - Mk. IX Spitfire.

Most war historians agree that World War II witnessed the very last of the "Knights of Battle". Those men who fought "Mono a Mono" against each other. Risking and giving their lives for their king, their country. Hand-to-hand combat on the ground had virtually disappeared — giving way, for the most part, to mechanized warfare — long-range artillery and pinpoint bombing from the air.

To most soldiers the enemy was "over there" somewhere. Usually unseen. Not so the fighter pilot. He was the final knight in the evolution of man fighting man. From stones, clubs, arrows, spears, swords and pistols — the fighter pilot evolved. The last knight of battle. In Word War I the first pilots flew observation account planes minus the guns. The pilots would often wave and salute as they flew by their "enemy" pilot. That soon changed when testy aviators actually "cast the first stone". Literally. In the early stages of the World War I, an observation plane, unidentified, actually dropped a large rock on the helpless enemy pilot flying beneath. It wasn't a "Kill", but it damaged the structural integrity of the fragile wood and linen wings on that early craft. Nor did it enhance the "stoned" pilots' affection toward his adversary. Soon stones were dropped by both sides, followed by bags of stones, followed by pistol and rifle shots and ultimately machine guns, timed to fire through the planes propellers. Thus was born the famous Knight of World War I: Baron Von Richothoven with over 80 kills; Billy Bishop of Canada, with over 50; American

Eddie Rickenbacker, 28; Mickey Mannuck, England's one-eyed ace of ace; Frank Luke, the famous balloon buster. These aces became national heroes during World War I and after. Particularly heroes to the youth. Books magazines and films whetted the appetite of young lads to fly — to some — day race their steeds through enemy skies, to find and to fight the enemy in glorious battle. Indeed ... like knights of old.

One of these was a young Canadian country boy named Jerry Billing from Essex, Ontario, Canada. Jerry read stories, saw the films and built models of the real thing. He didn't know how or when, but he knew he must. Who would make it possible for a poor Canadian country boy to reach that unreachable dream? One man could — and ultimately would. A failed Austrian house painter with beetle mustache and a crazed vision of a thousand-year reign for the Third Reich. An unlikely dream maker with the unlikely name of Schickelgruber...Adolph Schickelgruber, also known as Hitler.

When the Luftwaffe covered Europe like a black cloud, the RAF was pitifully overmatched. Volunteers were called upon to come to the aid of the Empire. Australia, New Zealand, South Africa and Canada responded with the alacrity expected. Also India, still a member of the Empire. Young men and women began flight training in DeHavilland Tigermoth and Fleet Bi-planes. Then onto Harbored Monoplanes and soon the fighter pilots graduated to the Hawker Hurricane, and some — if they were lucky — ultimately to the queen of them all, the British Supermarine Spitfire. The English designer Reginald Mitchell, had obdurately, steadfastly argued that the "Spit" was the only Allied fighter at that time that could compete with the proven and vaunted Messerschmitt 109 — to say nothing of the Focke-Wolf 190 about to leave the German design boards. America had shifted her factories into a military gear, but was yet to make a firm commitment to join England against the hated Hun. Pearl Harbor was over a year away.

The young Canadian immediately enlisted. Barely out of high school, Jerry Billing started at the very bottom. Or so he thought, until he and another buck private were arrested for assaulting a camp sentry box with fixed bayonets. At the hearing that followed, the 18-year old explained that he wanted action, that he wanted to fly for his country, and would do anything for the opportunity. The judge was impressed, gave Jerry the necessary test, and Jerry was soon calling his eight brothers and sisters with the glorious news: he was in flight training.

Soloing in the open cockpit, Fleet primary, he soon advanced to the Yale French plane, and then was off to England to fly the Hawker Hurricane fighter. Soon thereafter the 19-year old pilot showed his outstanding abilities, and ultimately his dream was realized when he climbed into the cockpit of the magnificent Supermarine Spitfire MK 1. But that was not enough for the young Canadian sergeant. He immediately volunteered for fighter duty protecting the beleaguered and battered island of Malta off the North African coast. Italian and German forces had isolated the island from supplies and whittled the small air force to virtually nothing. Twelve intrepid Spitfire pilots soon took off from the British aircraft carrier *Furious* for a 1,200 mile over-water flight to the small island. One plane and pilot was lost on take-off. Ammunition and food supplies were extremely meagre. Food consisted of

Bully Beef and Hard Tack laced with maggots. Fighting was relentless with Messerschmitt 109's and Italian Macchi fighters attacking daily. The young fighter pilot was at last getting what he wanted: the most intense air combat of the war. Constantly outnumbered, Jerry and his teammates scored incredible victories.

Normal tour of duty for Malta was four months maximum. The young Canadian insisted on staying on. Finally after seven and a half months of continual air combat — scoring many kills and being shot down twice in the Mediterranean — the young Canadian reluctantly returned to England where he flew Sorties and "rare dog fights" over France; kills were scored along with destruction of the dreaded German VI launch sight. During this time, the young flight sergeant never bothered to apply for the four upgradings in rank for which he was entitled. Back in England Steve Randall recognized this oversight and Jerry Billing was finally made Flying Officer. All Jerry wanted was action. He continued to get it.

D-Day at Normandy, 6 June of 1944 was the massive Allied invasion. Jerry was in the thick of it. On the very first day he destroyed yet another German, no balls, VI launch sight. The following day his Spitfire MK IX guns blasted a JU 88 aircraft over the beachhead. On July 1st, 1944, Flying Officer Jerry Billing, now finally with an RCAF squadron, was shot down by enemy anti-aircraft fire over Carantan Marches. Crash landing his Spitfire, Jerry eluded the Germans for one month by lying in the mud, between eating grass and an occasional cabbage, and skulking at night through the German lines. Finally Jerry met an elderly French farmer, a veteran of World War I. The farmer secreted him from the enemy in the town of Bréhal. Ultimately the entire town of 2,500 people protecteed the young Canadian until he was finally rescued by American troops weeks later.

Back in England, Jerry insisted on more action to no avail, the young hero was sent home to Canada to teach other young pilots. For all that country's great pilots potential, it is unlikely there will be many to fill the flight boots of Flight Lieutenant Jerry Billing. For he continually gave, without whimper, his all to his country and to free peoples everywhere.

I salute Jerry Billing. A magnificent pilot, a brave and great patriot, a treasured friend, and one of the last true Knights of Battle

4 / A Knave Among Knights in their Spitfires

Jerry's family coat of arms along with his decoration.
Notice the knight's helmet in the crest.

Acknowledgments

Rebecca M. Meluch, author in the Cockpit of the Spitfire Mk. IX.

I have kept records since 1939 which have been compiled into some semblance of ord r by Rebecca Meluch. She has laboured over this material for hours and hours My thanks go to Rebecca. Cheers.

Thanks must also go to Penny and Arnold McIntyre, Patrick McIntyre and to Jar Weir for their assistance in having the pictures included in this book.

Special thanks must go to a great Spitfire Pilot - S/Ldr. Dean Dover DFC / Bar for his assistance in having this book published. Without his aid I'm sure this story would not have been told. Dean was on another squadron than mine, but this does not mean we were not in the same sky while fighting the "Black Horde". A great pilot, a true friend and honoured acquaintance.

Dean Dover with his wife Joan.

Foreword
by
I. F. Kennedy
DFC & Bar

*I. F. Kennedy, DFC & Bar ex. C.
0. 401 Squadron, R.C.A.F.*

A Knave Among Knights in their Spitfires is the unembellished tale of a Spitfire pilot in the Second World War. I can vouch for its veracity: I was flying not far from Jerry Billing when he was shot down the second time in Malta, and was right alongside when he got knocked down by flak in Normandy a year and a half later. But, in spite of being shot down three times, Jerry kept coming back for more. Like his chum Don Goodwin, he didn't give a hoot for recognition or promotion; his only interest was tearing into enemy aircraft, strafing transport or E-boats, and generally attacking with gusto everything in sight.

Actually these fellows were not knaves: rascals, perhaps, on the ground, but knights in the air, true fighter pilots.

Jerry has been an exceptional pilot — his record attests to that. I can only mention a few of his achievements. After two tours of operational flying he taught fighter tactics on Sabre jets in post-war RCAF, test-flew supersonic jets for two years in England, was a test pilot for DeHavilland demonstrating multi-engined aircraft throughout Europe, and ferried aircraft to Vietnam. He continues to fly one of the world's few remaining air-worthy Spitfires at airshows in Canada and the U.S.A., and in 1992 received congratulations from the Queen for flying a Spitfire for 50 years.

"Scramble Red Section, Jerry!"

Comment

by Bruce (Steve) Randall

Steve, an exceptional Spitfire Pilot, completed 2 tours of operations against the enemy in W.W. II. He was never recognized for his exploits. A common fault for Fighter Pilots. Steve was eventually shot down over Europe to become a P. O. W.

This is a true story of intrigue, bravery and friendship. I met Jerry on the flight deck of the aircraft carrier, *Furious* in 1942. We were to fly Spitfires from the mid-Mediterranean Sea to Malta, which we did. This, in itself, was excitement but nothing to what Jerry was to experience later.

At one point, I saw him struggling in the sea after being shot down. He survived that. At another time, he was again shot down in Normandy and escaped after many life-threatening escapades.

Later, I was playing poker in the mess tent in Normandy when a voice behind me said, "Raise it." I looked around and there was Jerry back from 'no man's land' ready to go again. We were together again as instructors at an O.T.U. in England.

Jerry's flying did not finish with the end of the war, as you will read. He should be recommended for the Canadian Flying Hall of Fame.

PROLOGUE

The Blitz of Malta 1942 was said by pilots of the Battle of Britain to be more severe and more deadly than was the Battle of Britain itself. Few of those pilots are still around as we are a bit thin on the ground these days.

Just to get into the war wasn't the easiest thing to do. It seemed to be reserved for those of aristocratic background or for university graduates. My family was on welfare, and I might have walked by a university once. It was a problem.

Whether one wants to believe it or not, it is a fact that pilots in Spitfire squadrons in the 1940s were of a select few. I was quite fortunate that in the RAF your ability was the most important thing, as opposed to one's university standing. So I flew Spitfires.

Christmas 1942 found those of us in 1985 Squadorn in Malta pondering if we should pay $75.00 for a chicken. We settled for a rabbit, costing $50.00, only to find when it was skinned that it had a long tail (a dog?) "Cook it up. We are hungry," we said.

Malta was surrounded for 1500 miles in any direction by our enemy, the Germans and the Eyties. Food, aircraft, fuel, ammo and pilots were all in extremely short supply, and the Island was dangerously close to defeat, for it stood as a great thorn in the side of Rommel in his quest for victory in the Mediterranean.

We flew our Spirfires in sections of either four or two in line abreast formation. Eight eyes or four eyes in this formation are far better for sky coverage or fighting defence than in line astern as found in Britian.

F/L Withy and F/L Atkinson (officers), myself and Al Laing (sergeants), made up a section of four. F/L Atkinson had been terribly burned in a crash back in the UK. His face had been completely "redone." His left hand formed a circle sufficient to hook the throttle, his right hand a claw to grasp the control spade grip. Eventually he was sent back to the UK, as the skin would not heal properly around the claw.

We were patrolling just west of the Island when I spotted a couple of E boats. We were actually looking for JU 52's. We half-rolled our Spitfires to attack. I turned slightly starboard; a beam attack would give me more of the target to shoot at.

The first boat I sprayed with cannon fire; the second and larger I gave cannon and machine gun fire. We banked and climbed sharply to port when I spotted three Eytie Macci's (202's) above about 3000 feet. One bitch was spiralling for attack, so I pulled the nose of the Spit up and gave him a long squirt from his port quarter. Puffs of smoke appeared when he passed over me.

I stalled as I fired at the second, calling my section to watch out for three more higher up. Atkinson broke quite sharply to the left. Withy veered to the right and began climbing. Al Laing just veered about, sort of lost.

Recovering, I dove and broke to port, bringing myself on the inside of Al. I called and said, "They are splitting up now. Two are going north, and the others are up-sun".

Laing apparently did not see them, so I immediately piped in again and said, "They're Macci's, I'm sure, the nose, tail and wings. Al, they are Macci's, all right."

Al must have twitched in his Spit as he said, "For Christ's sake, Billing, where are they? Where?"

Well, I said to myself, he must be blind. I replied: "Hang on to my tail, Al. We are going up."

Just then Atkinson radioed, "I think perhaps we'd better join up and go home. Check your fuel."

Checking, I had to agree, as we still had some 98 miles to fly to Malta.

I dove, throttled rapidly, did a screaming turn up into the sun, saw one of the bloody Eyties, and gave him a long burst from astern quarter, seeking strikers along the entire fuselage. He then toppled off to the northwest, probably to Pantelleria.

No claims were made for these attacks — although strikes were made on both Macci's, one emitting smoke — because no one was free to view the strikes. In the RAF in World War II, confirmation of a "Kill," "Probable," or "Damaged" must be made by another pilot or cinefilm. The latter we didn't have, as we were only fortunate to have fuel and ammo and food; and the former was usually as busy as you were. Characters in the movies and some exaggerating types say they watched as the enemy turned, broke into flame, hood off, bale out, etc. Any battle I was in, you shot, saw your strikes very briefly, then broke like hell to ensure no one was behind you — as invariably you were separated from your friends once the attack began and you would be stupid to make yourself a sitting duck.

In the RAF a Kill was only given if you had a witness. A Damaged claim was given when witnessed and each saw damage but the aircraft was not seen to blow up or crash. A Probable was when witnessed and the enemy aircraft appeared to be hit but no damage was seen, or good damage and the E/A was assessed unable to return or sustain flight.

To destroy an aircraft on the ground was never considered a Kill, and how could it be, with no one in it? The Yanks, Germans, and Russians all recorded this type of destruction as a Kill. RAF claims would have been wild if we could have counted aircraft not airborne.

We returned to the Island without any success that would be put on paper.

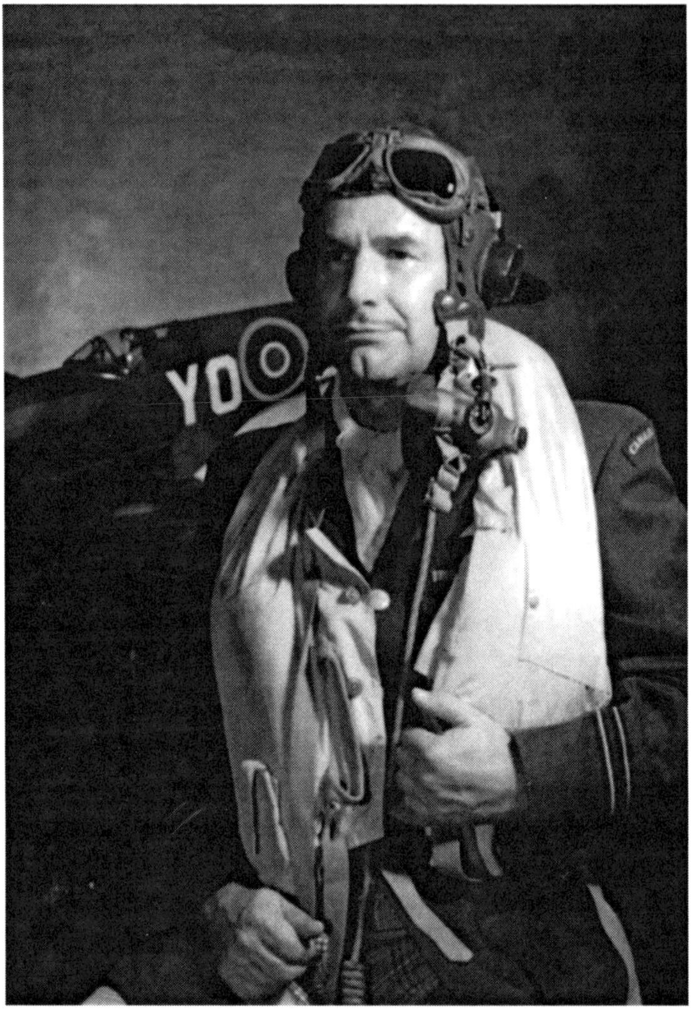
YO

1. PREWAR DAYS AND ENLISTMENT

The late 1930's found me in the most sunny portion of Canada, living with my parents in the small town of Essex. Activity there was almost nonexistent with the Depression days and everyone desperate for money. I came from a large family, five sisters and three brothers, one sister being my twin. I suppose I became conscious of the outside world and its vast expanse when I was sixteen years of age. In 1938, after Franco's victory in the Spanish Civil War with the aid of Hitler's Luftwaffe, when England was rearming itself in earnest, I wrote to the Royal Air Force (RAF), for I wanted above all to be a pilot within that organisation. The words "Royal Air Force" held for me a power and an excellence that today I cannot fully express. The reply that I received simply stated that they were pleased to hear of my interests, however my age did not warrant further action.

Late in 1938 I wrote to the RCAF in Trenton, Ontario. They were quite blunt and said that I did not have the required education to entertain an interview.

My family was at this time on welfare assistance. I remember clearly at Christmas time they would give you a tub full of food as a Christmas present, and in that tub were socks. My sisters would get these long socks — only they were bright red. The only people who wore these socks were people on welfare, and the girls were very hesitant to wear these bloody socks. It was a tell-tale deal. They would rather freeze and have red legs than have red socks.

While attending grade school I was obliged to miss class to take up the end of a shovel for my father, who was one of a group detailed to dig a sewer ditch in repayment for the welfare which the town of Essex was giving us. How clearly I recall the welfare investigator who used to look at our bread box and even count the loaves. I remember the day my mother tried to explain where all of the potatoes came from, given to us by a farming uncle. She was most religious, but I'm afraid the food problem came first that time.

The purpose of my being on the end of the shovel was so that my father could sneak off and earn a few nickels somewhere. In this way the chap in charge of the group could truthfully say that Billing was on the end of the shovel that day.

That fall I obtained a position from Eddie Michael as manager of a bowling alley by day while playing hockey and basketball by night. From these sports I learned that I could do, if I wanted to, most anything without too much effort. There were two older and more experienced bowlers whom I could actually toy with and select any pin at any time and have a final point of one or two above, absolutely upsetting my opponents so much that they refused to play again.

I used to read countless books of the World War I pilots. When I was eleven years old I received a small model plane and hangar for Christmas. My love for this was so great that I still have this set today.

I built an aeroplane in our back field, made from slats of wood and covered with burlap. I watched bugeyed as four local men, Len Bedal, Jim Witson, Gord Robinson and Stan King, built a "Sky Camper" in an old barn outside of town. Ford

TRAINING - PRIOR TO W.W.II

The stories of " AIR FIGHTING " in W.W.I was to me " Terrific ", -
The Spanish War was frustrating to me; " Finally " -
W.W.II and my chance to enter ...." GREAT ",!!!!!!

Motor Company gave them a Model A engine, free. The first flight was OK, but on its second flight it struck a telephone wire. The machine was pulled back into the barn and left to rot. I spent endless hours peering through the cracks in the barn, terrified that I would be caught. Even then it was my main ambition to fly and to have my own airstrip.

Today Len Bedal has his own aircraft parked at my back door. Jim Witson and Gordie are both deceased.

The Windsor Star used to have a single-line comic strip, and daily I would read the life of the three characters (Slim, Doc and Curly). Other books on air fighting which I read told of G8 and his Dare Devil Aces. My stock of these was great, and I would read them over and over again, and never find them boring. In those days the local library was lacking in this type of material, and I was always in search of other sources.

By the end of 1939 most of my friends had left, all of whom were a few years older than I was, having joined the Essex Scottish Regiment. So they beat the wolf at the door, only to be demolished at Dieppe in 1942.

At that point I could not relish the prospect of trench warfare. I was still too young, but I refrained from visiting the downtown area too often. My friends were gone, and I have always had two distinct fears — one of being branded yellow, the other of losing my faculties.

For one year I tread water. Reading became a top priority. I could not acquire enough material. I would lower a book from the library's rear window, then return it a few days later and acquire a replacement. The old grouch of a librarian did not appreciate my presence in *her* library and was always relieved when I left. I was a rags type and not too clean. I suppose it follows that I possibly smelt too ...

I had followed the news of the Spanish Civil War with great interest. The 1940 Battle of Britain for me was no less than wholly frustrating. By autumn 1940 I had personally received three letters from the RAF, all giving me the same reply. However, in late October 1940 I received great encouragement. The RAF would interview me "if" I could make myself available in Britain. No one can realize my plight at this time — "broke and poorly clothed," with no prospect of any type of employment to assist.

I questioned everyone on the possibilities of arriving somehow in the UK. A dockworker on the Detroit River suggested working my way over on a boat, but I would have to travel to Montreal to sign on. That was as much a problem as it was to travel to Britain. I was simply at a low point during the fall of 1940.

In November 1940 I saw a recruiting sign in Windsor for the RCAF. My age now was no problem, so I applied. The recruiting officer gave me all the required forms and medical exams; one being trying to balance a pencil-type metal stick on a flat plate out to arm's length and back, a feat I easily accomplished to the great astonishment of the medical man. The outcome of the interview was that I did not have the education to become a pilot, but I could qualify as a straight gunner. I immediately accepted. It was my chance at least to get to England.

I departed Windsor and arrived by train in Brandon, Manitoba prior to Christmas 1940. At the time I was wearing only thin-soled Oxfords with cardboard in my shoes, and a light threadbare coat. It was twenty degrees below zero. The pleasure I experienced upon being issued woolen socks and clothes plus a pair of the first overshoes that I had ever worn was terrific. It was terrific. I was even able to eat all the food that I wanted and still found more available.

Training for the next few weeks was little more than exercises in discipline. I entered the wireless class (Morse Code) and became so proficient in two weeks that they changed my rating to "Wireless Air Gunner", which was a step above "Air Gunner". Because of my persistent demand on the training personnel to accept my qualification for pilot, I was called in before the Commanding Officer on two occasions. Finally the CO informed me that if I could pass a test in mathematics I might be able to change. From then I spent every spare minute with algebraic problems.

Some of the chaps with whom I had become acquainted at that time were Jack Adams of Cornwall, "Muskrat" Bye of Owen Sound, and Horney Roberts of Montreal. One night, while on guard duty, the four of us with fixed bayonets used a sentry box as a target, and for a half an hour charged the post, cutting its sides to ribbons. The officer of the guard was so upset that he put us on a detail of digging a sewer drain. This drain happened to run outside of the CO's window, and, as we were digging, he looked out and recognized me. I was taken off the detail and brought in before him, mud and all. He pointed a stern finger at me and said, "I will tell you what I am going to do. I like your spirit. The math professor will give you a test to qualify for pilot selection, and by Jesus, you'd better be good."

"I said, "Yes, sir", smiling, confident but nervous.

I completed the exam and was accepted. The load off my shoulders was terrific, and I could hardly wait to start.

As for my three confederates in the seige of the sentry box, Jack Adams was discharged early from the RCAF; Horney Roberts and Muskrat Bye completed their training and joined Bomber Command as "Gunners". They were both shot down over Europe.

'I said to the man who stood at the gate of the year...'

H.M. THE KING
BROADCASTS TO
THE NATION ON
CHRISTMAS DAY
1939

15 / Chapter 1

Department of National Defence
"Air Force"

IN REPLY PLEASE QUOTE
NO. 27-6-B

Windsor, Ontario, October 9th, 1940.

Mr. Gerald D. Billing,
Essex,
Ontario.

Dear Sir:

    This letter is to advise you that your application for service in the Royal Canadian Air Force for flying duty under the British Commonwealth Air Training Plan is much appreciated and has been recorded.

    As many inquiries have been received regarding applications from those who have volunteered for service in the Royal Canadian Air Force, the following information is offered.

    It should be understood that the Air Training Plan is based on a progressive development which will take some time to bring to complete fulfilment. The orderly development of the Plan provides that men be called up for duty as and when they are required, and does not permit men being called up for duty immediately following application.

    To ensure equal representation throughout Canada, recruiting quotas are allocated geographically and only a limited number can be selected periodically from each locality.

    Your offer of service having been recorded, you will be called upon when the opportunity offers. It must be pointed out, however, that any tests you have taken or medical examinations you have passed successfully do not guarantee final acceptance, and you should not, on any account, sever your civilian connections until actually called up for duty.

    The Air Force will, in all probability, require the services of the great majority of those who have applied, and the absorption of selected applicants will take place as vacancies occur.

Yours very truly,

MEDICAL F TESTS COMPLETED IN SEPT 1940

(C.L. Arnold) Flying Officer,
C.O., RCAF Recruiting Centre,
Windsor, Ontario.

Nat. Def. B-440

Jerry Billings reply from the Department of National Defence on his request to fly in the Royal Canadian Air Force 1940.

2. TRAINING DAYS IN CANADA

Because of my change to pilot status, I became separated from the original group of fellows and joined others in London, Ontario, my first air station for Elementary Flying. Adjusting to the routine of ground school in the A.M. and flying in the P.M. was easy. I was amongst the first group to solo, and found that aerobatics were a treat. One instructor, who loved landing in small unauthorized fields and who taught me much about wind and its effect, was Max Harris, presently living on Pelee Island.

While in London we were flying Fleet Finch aircraft. The Fleet Finch to me was an easy aircraft; nevertheless I had trouble doing rolls. So one day for two hours straight I did rolls. Finally I was ill. What a mess. When my instructor was told the story he was simply amazed. But I mastered the roll.

The end of the summer found me in Dunnville, Ontario. In the Dunnville service school most of our flying was on Yales. The Yale was a tinny, noisy thing to fly, with only a lap strap for a harness. The aircraft were built in the U.S.A. for the French Air Force, but when World War II arrived they stayed in North America. The instruments read in European measurements, i.e. metres and litres, and the pilot had to work some division to acquire his height in thousands of feet.

One Yale I flew in mid 1941 was #3430. This particular aircraft now rests in the Air Museum in Winnipeg. To see the very airplane one trained on for war now quietly housed in a museum as a part of history makes one wonder: How archaic can one get?

In Dunnville my instructor was a Sgt. Pilot named Metcalfe, who excelled in low flying and aerobatics. He was later killed on Typhoons while engaged in ground strafing in Europe. To my surprise Metcalfe soloed me after only two dual trips on the Yale aircraft. Because of this I was two weeks ahead of the course in flying, but just keeping up in ground school.

The graduation exams hung over my head as a threat. Each previous class had taken care of this problem by entering the office of secured papers and obtaining copies of the exams the night before. Of course this meant burning the midnight oil prior to writing. This time however the heads of the school found out about the exam stealing and planted a different set of papers in the office prior to our final exams. They must have smiled when they saw everyone's face as the word was given to turn over the questionnaire and begin. Really, my heart jumped, and naturally I became nervous, but actually I found the test simple. Perhaps, as I recall now, the ease of it may have been due to my great interest in flying and determination to master the ground nonsense.

With all of the theory problems complete, I now entered the final stages of flight tests. Sgt. Metcalfe asked me what I would like to be: Bomber, Fighter, or Instructor Pilot. This surprised me, for I thought he knew what I wanted. I had filled in my preference at the completion of each phase in training. We were asked to rank our choices in order. On the first line I had written 'Fighter Pilot'; on the second line, 'Fighter Pilot'; and on the third line, 'FIGHTER PILOT'. When I told Sgt. Metcalfe that I wanted fighters, he stated flatly, "Well, I am sorry, but you are slated to become an instructor and get your commission, and you will be based in Canada."

This was not what I was here for. For me, as a youth, because of World War I, a German — a Hun, a Kraut — was the worst enemy anyone could have and I really relished the thought of being able to face him, and before the age of twenty to be given wings and gun to kill him with full authorization and the blessing of all, no questions asked (But not old enough to enter a pub!). My motivation due to my surroundings as a youth certainly placed me well for battle. Staying in Canada, teaching others to fly instead, was utterly out of the question.

For Sgt. Metcalfe it would have been a feather in his hat to produce instructor material. I had other ideas.

My instrument test was soon upon me. This was an exercise whereby you are positioned in the rear cockpit of an airplane (a Harvard), with a light cloth covering the area about your head, forcing you to fly solely by instruments. I was to fly a triangle type cross-country to end up at the point of commencement. My plan was to screw this up to a point where I would be obliged to have a re-test. This I did, and when Sgt. Metcalfe heard of the test results, he was furious. In fact he screamed at me and said, "Get your flight gear!"

He put me in the rear of a Harvard, and for more than an hour and a half he flew the aircraft in continual aerobatics, saying, "That was a rotten trick, and I will make you so sick you will be sorry".

When finally he began to call out, he asked me, "Have you had enough"? Do you want to go back?"

Actually I was enjoying it and had become quite familiar with the flick (or snap roll, some call it), a torque roll maneuver. I answered him, saying, "Do you mind if I try some?"

I can still see his head jerk and look back around. "O.K., damn you, go ahead."

We returned and, on jumping down from the wing, he came over and said, "Jerry, I'm sorry. Have fun and I will make sure you get your fighters."

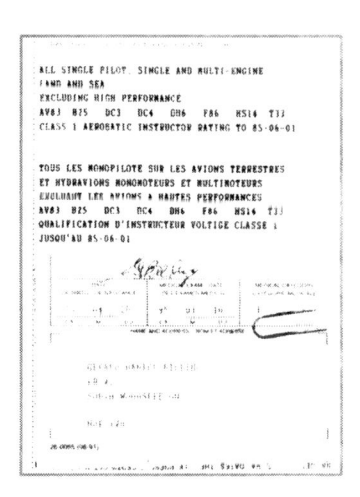

3. OVERSEAS OPERATION TRAINING

Never having travelled before but knowing of the Quebec French and their unwillingness to fight in World War I, I was aware of the atmosphere in that province, so, to no surprise, the Quebocois stoned our troop train as we passed through the small villages en route from Toronto to Halifax. We were told if you go into town in uniform to go in pairs.

My first ocean voyage came in December, 1941 on board the *Andes*. I joined a group of other pilots from the States who had enlisted in the RCAF, Godson, Peters, Pierce, McKinnon (a great pianist who entertained us across the Atlantic), Cisco Cobas, Moss Fletcher, Mike Askey, Pete Peters, Goody Goodwin, Pete Carter, Ray Fuchs, Red "Scarlet" Schewel, Babe Fenwich and Lloyd Brown. (All are dead except Cobas.) The trip across the Atlantic was terrible, taking seven days. We docked at Liverpool and moved by train to Hastings on Sea.

One point of interest that had always been present in my mind was that the clan of Billing at one time came from Britain. They apparently were seafaring folks, with great love for travel and vast spaces. One of the clan strayed to the Southampton area and founded the Supermarine Aviation Works at Woolston on the Itchen River, near Southampton in the year 1912. This chap was named Noel Pemberton Billing. There, R.J. Mitchell designed his S.4 monoplane seaplane racers which led up to his design of the Spitfire.

I arrived in the south of England at a holding area for Commonwealth aircrew. While there I had my first glimpse of a Spitfire Mk I as it made a low pass along the coast. The sound of the shrill whistle was to remain with me to this day. (This whistle is produced by the air rushing through the intake.)

Two weeks later I arrived at Tern Hill, an advanced flying unit having Master I's and II's along with the mighty Hurricane aircraft. My first impression of the Hurricane was that it appeared to be sitting with a hunched back, rather high off the ground, with a very heavy wing. For the next two days I spent hours around and in the cockpit of this aircraft, but in order to fly it, I would have to take dual instruction in Miles Master Trainer. I was given two trips in a tired, oil-dripping Miles Master Mk I. The windscreen would be covered with an oily film even after fifteen minutes of flying. My instructor was a pukka, ruddy faced Sgt. Jones who wore a terrific red handlebar mustache and spoke with a frightfully efficient British accent. This accent held me so entranced that I really never knew what the hell he was saying half the time. During our flying he would always say something that sounded like, "Wizz-ad." Of course I thought my flying was wrong and I would ask if I could to it again — a roll, a loop, or a landing. This "Wizz-ad" really had me upset, he said: "Looks like you will be one of the first to fly the Hurricane on the course." I asked him to please explain my problems in the air more clearly so that I might try and improve. His replay: "Oh, I say, old chap, you have absolutely no problems. In fact, your flying is absolutely wizard." Not until then did I recognize the bloody word!

He signed me out in the Hurricane, saying, "Press on, old chap, and have a jolly."

The cockpit check. I sat in the machine and found it to be quite comfortable with forward visibility excellent. The take-off was straight forward and easier than in the Yale I had flown in Canada. Flaps and undercarriage selectors were in an H form in one compact unit, one side for flaps and the other side for undercarriage. The throttle mixture and aircrew control were in the usual position, easy to reach with the left hand. Acceleration was much more lively than in anything I had flown to date. My first flight in the Hurricane was terrific, and once in the air I enjoyed a full hour of aerobatics. I climbed to 5000 feet and ran through slow flight, turns and stalls. Satisfied with this, I climbed to 12,000 feet and tried a spin. The Hurricane spun quite easily with positive recovery. I was amazed at the loss of height though, and made it a point to keep speed while doing aerobatics. Aerobatic maneuvers were a pleasure, with rolling a bit heavy I thought.

Flying had at last become exciting. Before one's eyes was the gunsight, and on the spade grip of the control column was the gun button — two things that I would enjoy for the next three and a half years.

Returning to land I found I had terrific forward visibility. I still recall my first landing and my thoughts: "What an easy aircraft to land."

Mishaps at the unit became quite frequent. On the first day a sergeant from the other course had an engine cut on final. He tried to stretch his glide, and the Hurricane flicked and went straight in. Sgt. Byrd on his first solo come in too hot and went hell for leather across the field, tearing the wings off at the far end and smashing himself up so much that it ended his flying career. Lloyd Brown, for some reason, come in hot as well and smashed into a wall, killing himself. We lost three pilots from our course, which lasted two weeks.

My one "problem" came during night fighter assessment. I wanted daylight fighters, Spitfires. For night fighter assessment we were asked to distinguish objects in a dark room from a viewing screen. I simply said: Looks like a cow, a house whatever, when destroyers, etc. were shown. I failed night fighter selection. Ha!

I completed advanced training with an above-average assessment and was posted to a Spitfire operational training unit at last.

Our flight commander was F/L F.W.M. "Frank" Jenson, a prince of a man and an exceptional pilot. F/Sgt Tony Parker was my instructor and quite keen to fly. Our group was divided into two flights. Mike Askey, Greg Cameron, Cisco Cobas and Gordie Bray were some of the pilots alloted to my flight. A quick circuit in a Master with Tony and he OK'd me for a solo in the Spitfire I.

My first impression on viewing the Spitfire was: Christ, what a terrific aircraft. She sits there with her nose high with an air of distinction — rather a proud dame, I thought — the wings quite thin with the tips tapering off to a sharp edge. I asked if I could sit in one prior to entering the F/Cmdr's office. Chills actually ran down my spine as I entered the cockpit and touched each control. To this day, fifty-two years later, I still get that feeling as I mount this aircraft (perhaps it is because the fuselage describes a woman's leg when viewed from above and behind).

I sat for several hours after ground school in the cockpit, as I wanted to have complete knowledge of the controls. Navigation in Britain is a far cry from

Spitfire Mk. II, 30 Gal. Tank fixed in wing

Gp. / Captain F. W. M. " BOSS " Jensen, CBE, OBE, DFC & Bar, AFC, AE, RAF. He was an instructer with Jerry on Spitfires Mk. I and Mk. II's

navigation in North America where the roads run North/South or East/West. Britain's roads and railways are numerous and define a spider's web. The possibility of becoming lost was paramount at all times.

I was ready for my first flight in a Spitfire MK I, Serial K 9929, one of the first initial order of 310 production Mk I Spitfires ever built. This Spit did not have the automatic undercart selection, but had a selector (up or down) and a long pump handle on the starboard side that the pilot had to pump until the wheels indicated either up or down for that selection. Everyone on the ground knew a first solo because when the pilot pumped the handle with his right hand, he invariably moved the control column at the same time, causing the aircraft to climb as though going up steps.

Taxiing was completely different because of the long nose and the position of the cockpit, requiring "S" turns at all times when taxiing. We were told to take off in a three point attitude because one could hit the prop if the tail was allowed to raise. Several pilots, in their desire to see ahead, did this very thing, only to chew their props (which were wooden) to pieces.

I opened up the throttle on take off, held the control column neutral and was airborne quite quickly, selecting up to clear the undercarriage. I then sat back and waited for this great speed. My I.S.A. read 140 mph, but I had expected to flash across the ground as I had seen that Spit do at Bournemouth. Really I was disappointed, possibly because of my recent Hurricane flying and the great caution of the instructors. However, after the first half hour, and after stalls, turns and a spin from 14,000 feet, I began to feel the gracefulness of this machine so much that I had extended my thirty-five minute authorized trip to about one hour and twenty minutes. I returned to the circuit with the recommended continued turn on final until landing with only ten gallons of fuel.

F/L Jenson, My O.C., complimented me on my procedure (a good feeling), for Jenson himself would beat up the drome daily, diving to become inverted between our Nissen huts, then pushing hard to the vertical position, stalling out to half spin and recovery with a half loop, pitch and land.

My acquaintance with the Spitfire became absolute as I would sit for hours in the cockpit, running over each item, drills, and speeds, until to this very day I have not forgotten and can place my hands on each item, even blindfolded.

One of the worst problems we had to deal with was the weather. Invariably the visibility would go down, low cloud would move in, generally with light drizzle. On one occasion I was caught out. I picked up the west coast of the Bristol Channel, following it along just above trees and buildings until I found a point in the river that would lead me to the aerodrome. I had to make two passes at my approach as fog had now settled into the trees. Half of the time my circuit was in the scud cloud and I simply held my height and turn, timing it sufficiently to start my next run. With my wheels down, fuel reading zero, I turned onto final and found that I had judged it right, as the end of the runway passed below my wings. Returning to the dispersal I found that we had lost three pilots. Two had collided and one went straight in.

F/L Jenson's greatest problem in those days were two sergeant pilots — Cobas and Billing. We would stay on the flight well after all the others had left, and plead for another flight. In the morning we were always there one hour ahead of the other chaps and would takeover his office, each sitting with our feet up on his desk. When he walked in, we could wave a hand casually to him and say, "Morning, Boss." This, in the traditional British Dispersal, never sat too well with him, until he accepted our antics and took both of us more or less under his wing. The flying he taught both of us (and this was extra after the others had gone to the mess hall) was great. Before we were half way through our course he had us doing close low level formation aerobatics, something that as yet had not been done at the O.T.U. Before we graduated the three of us would put on a special show for the whole station. A terrific man.

On graduation I found another side of the station, this being the bar in the mess. Until this time I had never frequented the bar. As a matter of fact, I never knew it existed nor had I asked. Mainly, I suppose, because I never had time. I simply ate my meals and went back to the aircraft or to my room.

Graduation was wild. I tasted my first mug of beer but never finished it. As the party was beginning to get rough I returned to my room and began to ready for my departure.

We were all asked where we wished to be posted. Canadian squadrons were available or RAF squadrons with Canadians mixed. F.L Jenson asked me if I would like to go to the top RCAF squadron at Biggin Hill, He said, "Your assessment's above average and you would fit in well."

I asked if he knew which squadron had the first Spitfire and if it was possible to go there. He said, 'I will ask and let you know."

He later told me, "#19 Squadron, and I can get you in, but it is a very mixed group, Czechs, Poles, Free French, etc."

I answered, "Please get me on it, would you?"

The next day found my train bound for Lands' End and #19 Squadron at Perranporth. As I sat in the train on that long journey I felt that I had finally accomplished what I had longed for years ago: the RAF and to actually be going on the first squadron with Spitfires.

Because of my selection, I became lost as a "colonial" amongst the aristocratic British. Pay, promotion, contacts, and the like would not catch up to me for over a year or more. But ability was always recognized as grounds for acceptance, and is something that the British still hold to very strongly.

As I recall, while on the train to Perranporth, Cornwall, I took off my Canadian badges and did not wear them on my shoulders again until I joined #401 Canadian Squadron in 1944. My main reason was to be as inconspicuous as possible amongst this new group and to be recognized as an RAF pilot. From the RAF stores I drew a pair of RAF pilot's wings that I wore until rejoining in 1948.

23 / Chapter 3

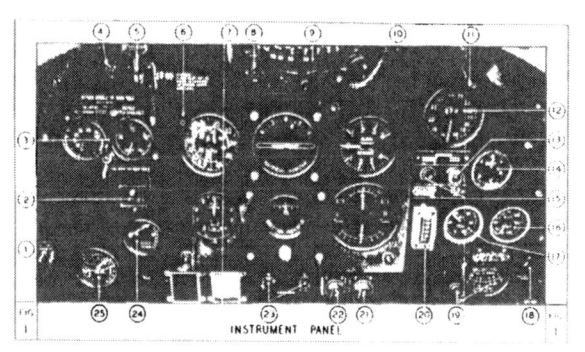

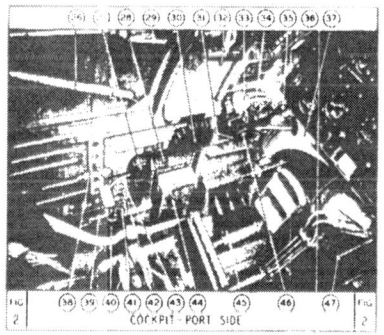

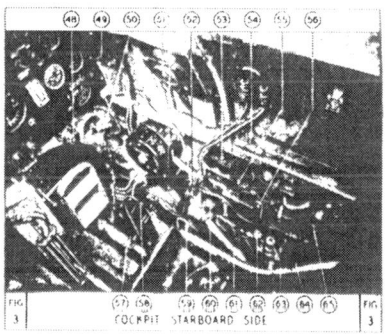

1. Ignition switches.
2. Undercarriage indicator.
3. Oxygen regulator.
4. Navigation lamps switch.
5. Flap control.
6. Instrument flying panel.
7. Lifting ring for sunscreen.
8. Reflector sight switch.
9. Reflector sight base.
10. Voltmeter.
11. Cockpit ventilator control.
12. Engine-speed indicator.
13. Supercharger warning lamp.
14. Boost gauge.
15. Intercooler protector pushbutton.
16. Coolant temperature gauge.
17. Oil temperature gauge.
18. Fuel pressure warning lamp.
19. Fuel contents gauge and pushbutton.
20. Oil pressure gauge.
21. Engine starter pushbutton.
22. Booster-coil pushbutton.
23. Cockpit floodlight switches.
24. Elevator tab position indicator.
25. Brake triple pressure gauge.
26. Crowbar.
27. Rudder trimming tab handwheel.
28. Pressure-head heater switch.
29. Two-position door catch lever.
30. Elevator trimming tab handwheel.
31. Throttle lever friction adjuster.
32. Floodlight.
33. Throttle lever.
34. **Undercarriage indicator master switch.**
35. Propeller speed control.
36. T.R.1133 pushbutton control.
37. Slow-running cut-out.
38. Signal discharger pre-selector control.
39. Signal discharger firing control.
40. Power failure lamp.
41. Radiator ground test pushbutton.
42. Supercharger ground test pushbutton.
43. Oil dilution pushbutton.
44. Map case.
45. Rudder pedal adjusting starwheel.
46. Propeller control friction adjuster.
47. Fuel cock control.
48. Engine priming pump.
49. Signalling switchbox.
50. Fuel tank pressure cock.
51. Remote contactor and contactor switch.
52. Undercarriage control lever.
53. IFF pushbuttons.
54. Harness release control.
55. IFF master switch.
56. Undercarriage emergency lowering control.
57. Rudder pedal adjusting starwheel.
58. Drop tank cock control.
59. Drop tank jettison lever.
60. Windscreen de-icing cock.
61. Seat adjustment lever.
62. Windscreen de-icing needle valve.
63. Windscreen de-icing pump.
64. Microphone/telephone socket.
65. **Oxygen supply cock.**

4. #19 SQUADRON 1942

In early May 1942 I arrived at #19 Squadron with little gear and a strong desire to get going. A chap called Bradley was the F/Cmdr. The CO was S/Ldr Davies. I was billeted in a quaint old English country home along with Free French pilots Rene Royer, Jackal, Leblanc and a Czech named Henderson. These pilots were the first that I began to be acquainted with on operations.

My first flights with the squadron were on the Spitfire Mk II with a fuel tank fixed on the port wing. The squadron was in the process of changing over to Mk V's when I joined.

One day I was scrambled with Rene Royer to intercept a plot from Brest. At 22,000 feet I saw what appeared to be a pair of FW 190's, but they turned back to France. That was my first glimpse of the enemy.

I flew a few convoy patrols, and, with Rene, did quite a few Rhubarb patrols off the Aldernay, Cape de le Hague area, strafing anything — and I mean anything — we saw. We attacked Brest Harbour with our Mk V Spitfires, and received much flak and several holes in our aircraft.

On one Rhubarb with Rene over Aldernay, Rene called that he spotted four FW 190's in two pairs abreast formation. He was most calm, being experienced, but I was quite apprehensive because we were several miles away from base and because in the dispersal the older chaps spoke often of a German Ace they called 'Montony' (his real name was Nowotny) and that he was flying the FW 190's with a great score. We were told that the FW 190's were in the Cherbourg area.

I closed to Rene, I suppose for protection, but with sufficient room to manoeuvre. The FW 190 was a very good fighter, faster than our Spit V's but not as manoeuverable. The Spit could out turn the 190. However, given a 190 in the hands of a chap like 'Montony' and a Spit pilot a bit slow, the 190 would excel. No doubt the firepower of our 20mm equalled the firepower of the 190, which itself was a larger aircraft with a round, radial engine. It was an aircraft that certainly got our attention.

After a couple of violent breaks we found our position a quarter astern to two of the 190's. I almost lost Rene in those violent breaks, blacking out momentarily. (I was making sure that I would be inside of Rene.) I had pre-selected the wingspan of an ME 109 on my gunsight, and never remembered to change this setting. I was simply too preoccupied. The 190 looked quite menacing to me, especially should this Ace be aboard. Because we were able to gain this quarter astern position I reckoned it could not be him, as he would have been much more aggressive. Perhaps they were new pilots.

Rene attacked first, while I did some wild weaving higher to cover our tails, and, on completing an inverted flat turn, saw Rene about to finish his attack. I called to Rene that I was coming in. As I pulled through to the quarter astern on the other 190, I saw Rene's 190 smoking and diving to starboard. At this point I was at 1,600 feet from my target and opened fire to about 1,300 feet, when I saw strikes and pieces of the 190 flying off the inboard portion of the port wing. I saw nothing more of the aircraft, as I broke violently in the direction that I last saw Rene. I joined up with him quickly. We both then set up a defensive circle to clear ourselves. The other 190's had simply pulled up into the overcast and disappeared.

All of this occurred within seconds and at low altitude of some 12,000 - 13,000 feet.

When Rene said, "OK, Beel, that was good, let's go home," I formed up and we entered cloud for some fifteen minutes, then descended to the sea, picked up Bolt Head and returned to base at Perranporth.

This was my first encounter with the enemy aircraft.

More scrambles took place with little action, and the endless convoy patrols were a tiring job.

On the 24th of June '42 I was scrambled with P.O. Cheek (with whom I later flew on 185 Squadron in Malta) to intercept a plot off the south coast of Land's End, England. The plot appeared to fade into the west northwest over the ocean. After thirty minutes of flight, Cheek and I returned to base.

A few days later we learned that the bogey had been a 190 pilot who had become completely disoriented from his base in France as he had been on a sweep to the Land's End area, and he'd landed his FW 190 at Pembrey, South Wales. The pilot was obviously quite lost. The weather had been very poor with rain and fog.

This incident gave Britain its first Focke-Wulf 190, a prize, as this was a new aircraft much superior to our Spit Mk V's. The U.K. had been planning a move to enter France and steal a FW 190. The German pilot saved us the trouble.

On July 1, 1942 we flew to Biggin Hill and had our Spitfires painted with white stripes to wait for the Dieppe raid. We sat in the sun while two German ships (large ones, the *Scharnhorst* and *Prince Eugene*) sailed straight down the bloody English Channel without being challenged. The raid on Dieppe never materialized and we returned to Perranporth.

On 15 July, Paddy Finucane, the Irish ace, had not survived his ditching in the Channel. It was a beautiful clear day, and we had heard his R/T of: "This is it, chaps," while returning from France. He simply came down for a landing on the water, levelling off beautifully. The wake of his slipstream parted the water and he bellied on. The aircraft came to a stop, dipped low at the nose, bobbed back up, then dove vertically down, and that was it. An oil slick marked the spot.

Paddy Finucane's prang alerted all of us to the possibility that the headrest, designed to help your neck in a crash (to prevent whiplash) may have been the reason for him not being able to escape his sinking Spitfire. It was agreed by everyone that, had be been trying to get out without undoing his parachute, the bloody headrest could very well catch the back of your seat chute and drag you under. Our next move was to tear off the headrest from our aircraft, and it became a normal thing to dispose of.

Having flown many hours now, with endless air combat, mostly on Spits, I began to hear the stories of Malta. I knew little of where it was or of the push from the south against the Hun. To me it was simply a place to find good action, as the Germans were being shot down in daily numbers. I knew that the island was being devastated worse than England in the Battle of Britain. Why not have a go?

On 27 July, 1942 I had been selected to go to Malta, however the CO changed this and sent Pete Peters. Pete had been flying in Spain early on and had gained valuable experience. Peter Carter was the second pilot to leave for Malta at that time. I was not too pleased with the CO for taking me off the Malta postings, but he said to take it easy; I would go next time, if they asked.

More sweeps and convoys and fun with Rene Royer in the air.

Rene, Jacko, Henderson and I went on a sweep one morning and we ran into very bad weather somewhere off France. Jacko and Henderson both went missing, while Rene and I, as usual, had paired up and arrived back at base, tired and very low on fuel.

In September, #19 Squadron was still flying clapped out Mk V Spits. We also still had some Mk II's with the fixed 30-gallon tank halfway along the port wing; it was a fixed unit in the wing that formed part of the structure. Then on the 27th of September we were told that #133 Eagle (Yankee) Squadron had lost all their Mk IX aircraft. This surprised us, for why should the Yankees' Squadron have Mk IX's instead of us?

The reason they lost all eleven (one turned back early — oil pressure) Spits was that they were escorting bombers over France and took a tailwind for a headwind. Breaking cloud they saw coastline and water ahead, instead of water and coastline. Obviously they were still over France.

We scrambled to assist and to search the Channel off Lizard Point and Bolt Head. Some R/T was: "I'm baling out." "I'm going into this field."

For two days with a raging Channel we looked for those clowns, but found none. They had missed the target by eighty miles.

In October '42, I was finally posted to Malta. I left #19 Squadron rather reluctantly, but keen to have a go in Malta.

I never saw Rene again. I heard that he was shot down a few weeks later.

While flying with #19 Squadron, one could get the feeling that these characters were intent on killing themselves. However their strong urge to survive and to evade the enemy flak was sign enough that they wished to be free to return for more fuel and ammo in order that they might harass and kill all of the enemy if possible. Men with names ending in -et, -re, -eux, along with -ek, yu, and -ski or -kow were extremely sound and aggressive pilots. Dedication and trust in each other was far above the average. I might have joined a Canadian squadron, but would never have enjoyed such company without the selection I had made.

Along with all of this I am quite proud to say that #19 Squadron had at one time such pilots as Johnnie Johnson, Douglas Bader - the legless ace, Roy Dutton, Peter Nash, and Clouston, before my time, but some of whom I was to know personally later.

Arriving at Lyneham aerodrome, an air transport base, in driving rain, I decided to go to bed early. Sometime during the night the bloody door blew open. Rain and a very wet drunken body blew in. He threw his luggage on top of me and groped for the light switch. A great deal of cursing took place until the lights came on, and, low and behold, Goody Goodwin stood before me with a crazy gin, saying, "Hi, old cock. Guess I am late."

I told him to go to bed and that I would see him in the morning.

I rarely frequented the pubs nor drank, as I wanted to be clear-minded. Goody made up for me.

The next A.M. I kicked Goody out of bed and said, "Come on, you dog, get up and we'll go and eat."

After breakfast we were walking through the streets of the station when I noticed the armament building. I told Goody I thought that we should try and see if we could be issued with a gun. To our amazement we each drew a .38 revolver plus ammo.

A bad move.

We were to take off that night in a large transport to fly to Gibraltar. How lucky we were for that! Because, as the evening wore on, Goody and I took over the sergeants' mess with our guns, shooting out the lights and trying desperately to pick off the one over the dart board. The station warrant officer appeared in the doorway. We both opened fire over his head. He quickly disappeared. So did Goody and I, out of the nearest window. Before I jumped out, I grabbed a handful of musical records; we should have music later, I thought.

We groped our way through the darkened station and found the readied aircraft. We climbed aboard the transport and settled in for the ride to Gibraltar.

As the transport was approaching Gibraltar I woke up to find that all of the records had been smashed, as Goody had been sitting on the pile.

Upon arriving at Gibraltar we were very hot, tired and hungry. Our group was directed to a large lorry covered with canvas. Goody and I sat up front with the driver, and we proceeded to our camp.

On the way I noticed a Spaniard pushing a fruit cart towards the city, and I told the driver to stop.

Goody followed me out, and, with my gun at the Spaniard's head, Goody began to toss fresh fruit to the other chaps in the lorry. The Spaniard was most upset, but firing one round over his head appeared to pacify him.

We gorged ourselves with fresh fruit, only to suffer violently the next day.

That night we were briefed on our proposed sortie. It was a great surprise to me to find that we had to fly off a carrier.

We were to board the aircraft carrier *Furious* and proceed down the Mediterranean to Algiers, then take off the carrier and fly three hours or more to Malta.

The Spitfire at this time was not designed for carrier operation. A fifteen degree angle on the flaps was needed to assist take off, but Spitfire flaps have two positions only — fully up and fully down — nothing in between. Neither did the Spitfire have the range for this mission. We were provided with a 90-gallon drop tank for the extra fuel, and we put small blocks of wood in our flaps to give us the fifteen degree take-off position.

It was a one-way mission nowhere to turn to if engine or aircraft problems arose over 1,200 miles to the surrounded, blitz-torn island of Malta which desperately needed our Spitfires for survival.

At this point Malta was being heavily blitzed, and the nearest point of friendly held territory was over 1,500 miles in any direction. I looked about at my colleagues, each with above-average intelligence and courage, each being virtually

28 / *A Knave Among Knights in their Spitfires*

alone, especially once combat commenced. Survival was one out of three, and odds terrific. I was blessed with a strong desire to fly and became involved in air combat. I readied my ship for the takeoff and flight.

If the wheels would not retract or if your extra fuel tank failed to feed, we were briefed *do not* fly to Africa.

Our launch position would be just fifty miles north of Algiers, which was held by the enemy. We were told if you elect to land in Africa, the Arabs will cut your balls out, sew them in your mouth and send you back, to be rewarded by their superiors for it. If your aircraft became disabled, you were to bale out well ahead of the aircraft carrier which would do a running pick up. Hopefully. We were made fully aware of the carrier's position, in that it could not stop to pick anyone out of the seas.

1987 - Jerry receiving Medal of the City of Brehal, France and Honorary Citzenship

5. MALTA BLITZ ('42 -'43)

On the eve of our scheduled sortie to Malta in October 1942, Goody and I stood on the carrier deck, I recall, both agreeing it was a joke and we would not be asked to carry the exercise out. The next A.M. about 0500 hours we found out differently. All the aircraft were on deck and ready.

Your luggage was in a parachute bag tied to the frame behind the seat where it swung by itself as you flew. At any rate, one of the chap's Spit would not start, so they simply cleared his aircraft by shoving it overboard. The chap really scrambled to save his parachute bag from going over with it. He returned to Gibraltar with the carrier to try again with the next carrier.

The order for take off from the *Furious* for me was aircraft EP 571 (a tropicalized Mk Vb) the sixth in group 4. During the take off of the second group, one of the chaps screwed his procedure in some way and went screaming off to the port, ending up in the drink.

I think this was the smallest aircraft bloody carrier they had. We could not see ahead of us, anymore than we ever could in a Spit taking off. We had to line up the port cannon with a yellow line on the deck and go. But these were not my major worries. By now the episode with the fruit had come back to haunt me again, and I was suffering terribly from dysentery, a plague we were to call "The Malta Dog." Prior to my take off I had to visit the lav on two hurried occasions. Strapping myself in the machine I felt extremely weak and very dry at the mouth. Looking out of the cockpit to the swaying diving motion of the ship and the sea around me made me feel even more ill, especially when I could not swim. My main thought was, "How can I last for three hours?"

Once aloft we were supposed to fly parallel to the Algerian coast past Bone and Bizerta, skirting Tunis before heading southeast to Malta. But once past Bone, I flew alongside the lead aircraft and signalled a turn to suggest that from here we should cut across the forbidden Tunisian area. He agreed, and our section set course directly to Malta.

In doing this we flew to the south of Pantelleria, thus avoiding being intercepted by the Huns stationed there. We had no ammo; extra weight was not good.

As we passed Pantelleria, we were told to make a decision to drop or keep our 90 gallon overload belly tank. Tuning in on the Gonda control frequency at Malta I could hear a hell of a scrap going on, so I decided to get rid of the bloody tank.

Several minutes later we began our long descent from 26,000 feet. At this point I began suffering from cramps. Oh no. Don't tell me, not now, I thought.

We were instructed to land as quickly as possible at Luqa because of a dogfight over Hal Far.

My desire to land was imperative. I pitched for landing, gear and flaps down with a vicious sideslip into the aerodrome, turned to the left off the landing path, unstrapped, brakes on, and with the Spitfire idling, bounded for the hedge. What a relief. Overhead I could hear the whine of engines and the burp of guns.

30 / *A Knave Among Knights in their Spitfires*

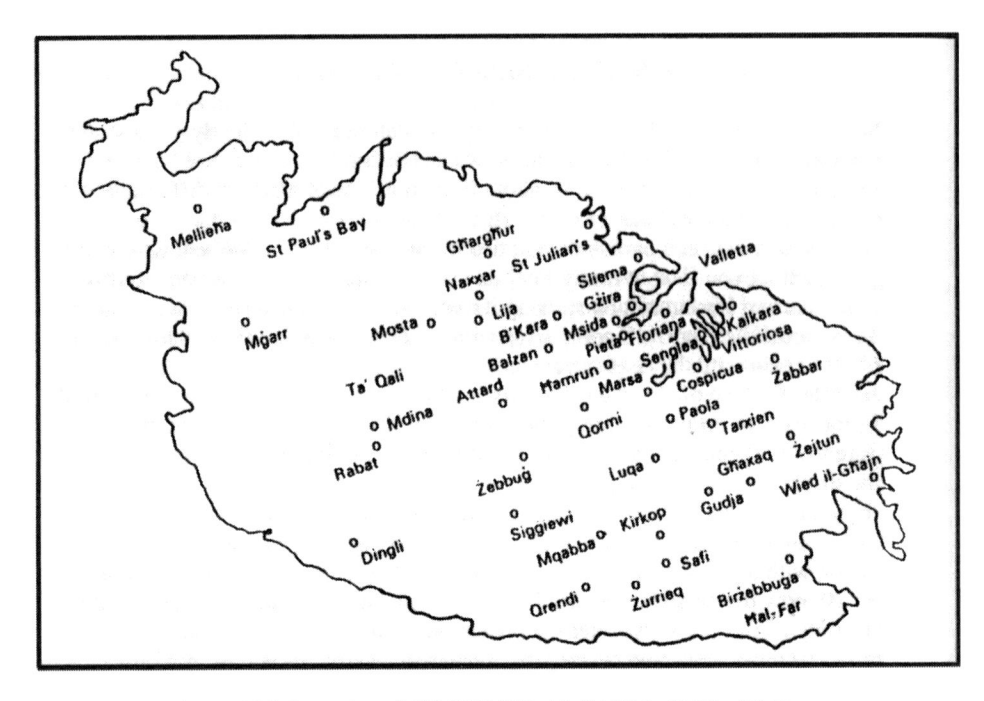

Map of Malta when " IT STOOD ALONE ", 1940 - 1943

Jerry in the cockpit of a Spitfire Mk. V, Malta 1942

What an arrival!

I taxied to the dispersal area where I was told to go immediately to the Hal Far drome, and within minutes I was on my way — and upon landing was pushed aside by everyone as they readied the Spitfire for an immediate sortie. No more than ten minutes had elapsed when the aircraft that brought me to the island was airborne to engage the enemy. My introduction to #185 Squadron.

We were met by Air Vice Marshall Park, a tall, lean, grayish-haired prince of a man. He shook our hands and said to me, "You appear keen and I know you'll have good hunting. Go, but keep your tail clean."

And he promptly departed in his Hurricane into the skies of Malta as a dogfight was in effect high above. Whether he engaged the enemy I could not say. However other pilots were arriving at other dromes — Luqa and Takali — from the *Furious*; perhaps he was roaring off to greet them also? We were all quite impressed with his great desire to fly and to participate at his age.

Hal Far drome was a dusty, one-direction strip, pockmarked to hell with filled-in bomb craters, short but usable. The dispersal was a soft limestone block structure, fly-infested, and hot running water not existing, with a smelly latrine, and everywhere with a typical tile floor — if you could blow away the dust. It was just a bloody primitive and make-do area, with lizards scurrying about the walls and everywhere else.

Housing was by means of taking over the homes of the local people who in turn would plunder and steal your belongings while you were at the drome some four to five miles away.

The Mess was a home that was set up sufficiently for us to eat what little there was. The biscuits we were given to eat were rock hard, and, you would knock them on your knuckle to rid the bugs from inside. But they tasted quite good, for we were practically starving.

No hangars existed, just five-gallon cans filled with sand and piled high around the Spit to protect the aircraft from bomb blasts.

But no one expected a scene as in the U.K. with lush green foliage and clean sheets with batmen for the officers. Hal Far was not really equipped in any form, but a makeshift operation everywhere. Actually I'm sure no one really cared what to expect for a war was on and what a terrific spot it was to be if fighting existed. The ground environment was the last thing on one's mind. Who really cared? The casual atmosphere as compared to the dress and tie nonsense was far behind. Very few types had the money to buy and wear a bloody tie anyway. And shoes? Shoes were something to wear, to hell with the polish — with all the dust!

There was, after all, a war on.

Some of the chaps on 185 were Major Swales, CO; Ken Charney, my F/Cmdr; Hal Knight, a South African; Al Ekert, American; Danny Hartney, Canadian; Johnny Miller of Toronto; a Captain Kuhlman, South African; Twitch Bollen, Mac Holden and Red Walker, all Brits. There was good old Len Cheek who always came home vertically and full power, Canadian; and Atkinson, who was burned hands and face losing all features. Also present were Al Laing, Gord Lapp, Matt Reid, Jeff Guy, George Mercer, Mac Maclaren, Carmody, and F/O Maynard.

32 / *A Knave Among Knights in their Spitfires*

The strength of " SPITFIRE WING " in Malta

Jerry 3rd. from right, checking oil screen on a Spitfire V. c, Malta 1942

Two days passed and I was to patrol an arriving convoy with an Aussie, P/O Park. We took off and stayed low level for quite a while, then set up a square search for the supposed convoy. I happened to glance at Park's aircraft when at that same instant his canopy flew off. He pulled up sharply and leapt out. I heard nothing on the R/T nor saw any other aircraft.

Being about 4,500 feet, he dropped quickly and struck the water without his chute opening.

Surely he must have been shot down, I thought, but there were no aircraft about. I set up a low cruise and circled him, calling "Mayday" on the R/T. Finally after what seemed like hours I was instructed to return to base, but I insisted that I was OK and that my fuel reading was good.

In the distance I saw the approaching rescue launch, and I led them to his body. I arrived at Hal Far and was told by my Erk that the refuel put in was the full amount that the aircraft held. I must have been flying on fumes. My first trip on the island of Malta.

The following day, led by Ken Charney, we were scrambled after twelve-plus 109's. There were four of us on the scramble — I was Number 2 to Ken — in line abreast battle formation.

It became typical: a melee that lasted some four to five minutes, then half roll and go home. Very brief and leaving one wondering: Where did they all go? One moment all hell broke loose, the next instant bright blue empty skies, sometimes broken by the sound of fire of an enemy A/C up your ass.

I was unable to get into position for a shot; however Charney claimed on the sortie.

On the 29th of October I took a trip to Takali to see old Red "Scarlet" Schewel, Pete Peters, Heatherington, Rip Mutch, Pete Carter, and George Beurling, some of the characters that I had known in Britain, now stationed at Takali.

Red Schewel from Owen Sound had been one of the guys at my training unit in Canada and we had arrived in the UK on the same bloody boat. When he saw me he yelled, "Billing, good, now we are all here. How the hell have you been?"

Pete Peters' comments were: "The food sure as hell is not like in Cornwall, England on good old 19 Squadron."

They had been in Malta longer than I had, and I was keen to find out from them about the enemy we were fighting. Red "Scarlet" Schewel advised me that the Eyties were prone to do aeros to try and outfly the Spit, while the Huns used the speed of the ME 109 E and F's to their advantage. The Hun would stay and fight. If he was experienced, then you really had to keep your arse clear or you've had it. Their 'climb to attack again' method of air fighting ranged from about 26,000 feet to the deck.

Scarlet was a fantastic pilot who survived Malta only to be killed eight months later in the UK when he flicked in while demonstrating evasive manoeuvers at low level in a Mk II Spit at an OTU. A great loss. Despite Scarlet's great fighting at Malta and with many, many dogfights behind him and many aircraft destroyed, he was never awarded any sort of decoration. Like everyone else — no one there to confirm. As sergeants, our main desire was to get the Distinguished Flying

34 / *A Knave Among Knights in their Spitfires*

The main street of Valetia after " Eyeties ", bombing, (Malta 1942).

M. E. 109 G, shot down over Luga, Malta, 1943. Tyres were made in the U. S. A.

Medal (a rare achievement), but he was never awarded anything. His record says he destroyed 6. And really everyone was in the same boat, for daily fights were the order of the day. Today some fifty years on, everyone tries to write abut Malta battles that no one recognized at the time. It's sad

In the UK decorations were given for completing sorties only. As in every battle, in Malta your unit became split up during the dogfighting, and it was every man for himself. One was too busy to see what was happening to your pals because you were too busy with your own job. If you saw a buddy in trouble, you would do your best to help. Most of the chaps who bought it were alone and standing off three, four, or more enemy at the time. *The whole episode took seconds*, only backed by guts and the great desire to compete. I guess one could simulate the Roman gladiator aspect, a prisoner with the desire to excel in a duel.

I stayed for a cup of chocolate and then left for the trip back to Hal Far, little realizing that, although I would speak to them on the R/T later, it was the last time I would ever see some of them again. Red Schewel was killed eight months later in the U.K. Pete Peters and Pet Carter were both shot down within the month. Heatherington and Rip Mutch were killed in the transport at Gibraltar in which Beurling managed to escape by diving out of the escape hatch. George Beurling joined 412 Squadron at Biggin Hill in 1944 a few weeks before I joined 401 Squadron, and was the only one of the old gang that I flew Ops with on my return to England.

George "Buzz" Beurling had 23 aircraft destroyed. He was the pilot who was rejected by the RCAF for lack of education but found that the British RAF was more knowledgeable in recognizing potential. He travelled via boat to the U.K. and excelled as a fighter pilot in the RAF, only to be claimed by Canada and the RCAF later.

I have read many articles concerning George Beurling and do not agree that this man resented a wing man of a Number 2 or that he was a "determined loner." Beurling's close friends were killed early in Malta or on Gibraltar. I personally know that losses like that create a deep hurt felling, and unless a person has experienced this feeling, he cannot know. I don't mean on one or two occasions where a close friend is killed, but on a continuous basis and almost daily. There is simply no way to share or express how one feels in the situation.

It is true to say that Beurling's close friends numbered few at the close off World War II, but that is because those who actually sat down to eat a meal or spend idle time with him just were not around anymore.

George loved to be able to pair up with another keen pilot and meet most any challenge in the air to prove his ability to command or get the upper hand. But once a man is saddled with other assessments, it becomes very hard to change the popular opinion of him. This fact holds true today. All that is needed is for one or two to draw attention to some trait — true or false makes no difference — of a person and it becomes gospel and is passed on to others.

Some writers of Malta have expressed views that the pilots of Malta were not clad properly in military attire. This was because both pilot and aircraft were extremely short of everything ... a war was being fought ... clothing, food, gas, all supplies were nil...

But George Beurling, Red Schewel, Pete Peters, Pete Carter, Heatherington, Williams — all, would, I know, be upset to have this man's assessment made of them. It is too bad they are not around to defend the statements. During my visit, George and Schewel were both dressed alike, and indeed I had the exact same attire, and to be told that our clothing was disgraceful would have been real fighting words.

I suppose one could get twitchy when each day consists of sitting in a Spit or in the Dispersal waiting for sudden calls to scramble. The ring of a telephone always demanded instant attention. But they complain of graceless manners?

All George wanted to do was to fly, to shoot down the Eytie and the Hun, and not to be bothered with unnecessary details. All everyone else wanted him to do was fly less, not to get too many Huns, for professionally he would then surpass the chairborne clots.

He was a professional, cool, precise marksman who found it unnecessary to have a crease in his trousers, his hair groomed, and shoes shined in order to defeat the enemy. Even if the ass was worn out of his pants, his skills were not hindered.

I recall one briefing early in 1944 at Biggin Hill, Buck McNair was running through a sweep that would take us away from Abbeville — for no reason better than it had been pre-planned — George stood up and questioned the route and why we were not taking in Abbeville. McNair said, "It's all right, George. We'll stick to the plan." Whereupon George said, "If that's the route, then I'm not going today," and promptly walked out.

George was right. We saw nothing on that sweep. However one squadron commander, Norm Fowlow, was blown to hell by a direct hit, point rounds of Ack Ack over France.

Why, if everyone believed that a war was on and that Eytie and Hun should be destroyed, did they not allow George and other great pilots to:

a) fly as often and as long as they wished?

b) shoot and destroy the enemy in any way possible?

c) take aircraft deep into enemy territory and blow the training schools and pilots to pieces?

d) dress in the attire in which they felt comfortable? (Some from the Depression era found ties and new clothes uncomfortable. The rich and first-class citizen never weighed this problem. How could they?)

e) fly only with who they wanted to fly?

To be led by an officer very often was dangerous as quite a few held the rank but lacked in fighting experience.

George's reputation (by the professional jealous types) of disregard for senior officers was only true if the senior types were inexperienced or lacking in aggressiveness.

Some writers have written that the reek of urine and vomit in cockpits existed.

What an absolutely ridiculous way to dress down this moment. No smell of urine or vomit ever came from the cockpit. Nothing but the sweet smell of oil and

37 / Chapter 5

185 Squadron, Halfar, Malta 1942. Williams - Eckert - F/L Atkinson.
F/L Atkinson was completely burnt about the face. After skin grafts he returned to England early with skin problems.

Jerry with other pilots in Halfar, Malta, 1942.
Geoff Guy U. K. (shot down by JU 88) - Red Walker U.K. (missing) - Danny Hartney Canadian (killed).

Mercer - Ekert - Jerry - Mc Laren (Halfar, Malta, 1942).

Jerry - Danny Harthey, Canadian, (Killed) - Red Walker, U. K (Missing) - Twitch Bolen, U. K. (Shot Down) - John Houlton, N. Z. (survived). (Halfar Malta - Blitz 1942).

exhilarating smell of glycol and 100 octane gas. They have no idea of the exciting moment or hours of readiness. Ask anyone who knows the smell of a Spit cockpit. It's terrific!

In 1985, I received a letter from W/C Prosser Hanks, CO in Malta '42: "Thanks very much for sending the book on Beurling. I have never read such absolute rubbish."

When a writer misses so thoroughly the character of this great effective fighting unit, its machines and men, I am sorry to know that the world will never capture the moments.

The next few days after my visit to Takali were engaged in patrols and scrambles which saw no intercepts.

The date is November 14, 1942, and about one of the most tedious jobs we have is our morning mil-run to the Linosa/Lampedusa areas to do our dive bombing show and then scout around and pray that we find an enemy transport plane. Eight of us would climb from takeoff towards the islands from Malta and, on reaching the islands, we would form echelon port and peel off to bomb, just as it's done in Hollywood, then climb up, look around and probably see half the bombs drop into the sea. We were very good at times.

We had absolutely no training for carrying bombs on a Spitfire. They simply put them on. The bombs were equipped with a three-foot rod attached to the nose so that they would explode above the ground and the shrapnel would travel a great distance. One simply did a vertical dive, placing the pipper on the target and release, then pull out of the dive.

Some bombs hung up to blow the tail off your Spit upon landing, so a rod was installed at the pilot's feet — one end resting atop the bomb, with a round two-inch plate at the top — as an emergency jettison device. The pilot simply kicked the bomb away — hopefully. I was never obliged to do this.

This particular morning we organized a patrol and bombing mission, our task being (a) to bomb the airfield at Lampedusa, and (b) to intercept a train of JU 52's scheduled to pass just west of Linosa Island. (So Ops thought).

F/Cmdr Withy and F/L Atkinson paired up. Dirty old Al Laing and myself, being sergeants, automatically stuck together through whatever happened. After the bombing effort (no one being too interested) we tooled off west of Linosa for the 52 train. These trains carried gasoline. If shot down, a huge fire followed.

Off to my left I spotted a of couple enemy boats. I reported them, and Atkinson says, "O.K., let's get them. Line astern."

Great, I thought. This leaves me tail-end Charlie.

They pressed on the attack. I gained altitude and veered off to starboard, leaving me in a much better position as this angle gave me sufficient time to rake both boats thoroughly.

As I passed over the last boat, I'll swear I'd hit it, I was so low. We banked and climbed sharply to port, positioning ourselves for another attack. That's when I engaged the Macci's flying high cover which Laing never saw.

The Macci's were flying in a loose gaggle, no similarity for defensive cover. I was climbing at full throttle as fast as I could. I pulled the nose of the Spitfire up

Maltese Farmer beside Spitfire- 1942

Spitfires on their way to Malta in the hold of an Aircraft Carrier 1942

41 / Chapter 5

A " Prang " by a pilot trying to avoid a recent bomb crater. (Malta).

Four Spitfires " Ready for Action " in Halfar, Malta, 1942

easily, while the other Macci's had seen me and began to turn. I easily turned behind the second Macci and closed to about 150 yards and opened fire. I took only one good burst and I was obliged to get the hell out because of the other Maccis.

Old Laing called me, and I thought he said, "What are they?" So I immediately said, "They're Maccis; I'm sure of the nose, tail and wings. Al, they're Maccis all right."

I guess I couldn't believe he was asking "Where? They looked like a billboard to me.

Al must have wrenched himself with disgust, as his aircraft twisted a bit, and he said to me, "For Christ's sake, Billing, where are they? Where" *Where?"*

I took off pieces of one and got a squirt in on the second before fuel forced us to turn back. I made no claims for these attacks. No one was free to view them, everyone concentrating on the bloody boats.

We flew back at about fifty feet over the water towards Malta, joining up with Withy and Atkinson. Withy, incidentally, claimed one Macci for the show. I didn't see that. I didn't say anything either. To scratch an officer's claim was asking to be posted to P40's in North Africa.

Near our destination it became quite hazy. Laing was on the extreme left, Atkinson, Withy, then myself all flying abreast formation. I checked my fuel and it read 10 gallons. I called the leader, Atkinson, and said, "I can't see the island yet. How about a fix from Gonda?" (our ground control), as it became damned thick now, and old Laing was barely visible.

We received a course, which I set, and I dropped down to a few feet above the water, hoping I could increase my visibility. I looked back to my left and saw my haven, Malta.

I called and said, "We just passed the island. It is about 8 o'clock to us."

Old Withy called and said, "I see it," and began turning immediately.

I knew damned well he didn't, but who was I to argue, being a sergeant?

I checked my petrol and it read five gallons. I called and said, "My fuel is quite low. I'll have to go straight in."

The answer: "You'll be O.K. Line astern."

To hell with this. I turned my radio off and decided to land first.

They approached the island then turned off for an orbit, so I throttled off, pitch full line, nose up, wheels down and dove a vicious slipping turn into my approach for a landing.

I landed well down the field and turned to my pen, checked my gas. No register. My Erk said I had two gallons of petrol left, not quite enough for a good drunk. I explained my situation, and nothing more was said.

On entering the dispersal, after talking to my mechanics, Laing took after me. "You son of a bitch, Jerry, don't you understand English? Where the Christ were they? I never saw a bloody one and you're giving me every detail. Why the hell didn't you tell me the colour of the Eytie's eyes?"

"Oh, horse shit," I said. "I thought you didn't know what they were."

The rest of the day was quite dull. We had a couple of scrambles and then stood down at noon. Al and I went to Slima, stayed all night, and came back the next morning to fly the afternoon detail.

We were given sweeps to Sicily and patrols over Grande Harbour, but no great action for the next couple of days.

The Eyties used a mixture of aircraft, Reggianes and Maccis, but also sections of only Macci 202's, mainly because they had a greater supply of Maccis.

The Reggiane was a good aircraft with low fire power, good turning ability, a much slimmer aircraft than the Macci. We saw few Reggianes about. The Eytie method of fighting was to execute aerobatics, an easy method to down a Reggiane or a Macci. One episode saw two Eyties run into each other. I find that in 1988 they had not changed their scenario, for in Germany their acrobatic team did a similar act. Non-habit-forming.

The Reggiane had an elliptical type wing and slender fuselage with an in-line engine, easily recognizable. The Macci 202 however had a snubbed, blunt nose, short fuselage which was also quite recognizable, and carried a wide white stripe around the fuselage ahead of the gun. The rudder also carried a white type of cross, marking it as Italian.

The Macci speed was much less than our Spit V's. The Macci had a radiator before the fuselage which stood out, it had a poor turning radius compared to the Spit V, and the fire power was low (machine guns), all of which made the Spit pilot a greatly superior aircraft. Most of the Macci pilots, as stated, simply went into an acrobatic routine, obviously not taught fighter tactics.

In general the Macci got to hell out and screamed for Sicily and home when intercepted. If the Macci had had a more powerful engine, it could have been a great deterrent for that side.

On one trip we were to fly top section of four for another section of Spitfires equipped with two 250-pound bombs, headed to Sicily. To me it was a ridiculous sortie because all the aircraft which we were protecting had to do was jettison their bombs to become fighters themselves. I was Number 4 and lagging behind when everyone half rolled for the attack.

As we headed back towards home, on passing the coast I was quite some distance behind when I spotted three JU 52's in close formation passing slightly under my starboard wing. I called the tally-ho but no one responded, so I simply continued the attack. I gave him a quick squirt and saw it flaming from the starboard engine. After firing at the first 52, I pulled up vertically, half rolled to starboard and pulled through with a ninety degree roll, placing me in a terrific quarter astern attack. Bags of time to settle the pipper on the wing root of the second JU 52. It always surprised me to see how slow the 52's travel. One could overshoot easily and you were obliged to throttle back until your attack was complete, then balls to the wall.

I called to the CO and said: "Come on, there is some fun back here."

Pulling up to starboard and entering some low clouds, I rolled back to port and was ordered by the CO to get back to the formation and that he was headed home.

I broke out of the clouds again and saw no more of the 52's.

No claims. No one to see.

44 / A Knave Among Knights in their Spitfires

Upon entering the dispersal — last — I found the CO really giving Johnny Houlton hell. When I had called the three 52's heading east and broke off, Johnny Houlton, also a sergeant, saw four 52's going west and attacked. The CO was most upset.

This was W/C. Thompson, who, although he was a Battle of Britain pilot who had won the DSO/DFC two years before, was not too keen now, burnt out in my estimation. He led a "Let's go over and get the hell back" sort of sortie. He really gave Houlton and me hell about dragging behind. Subdued, I said nothing of the encounter with the 52's, never even tried to claim. A posting to Africa, the hatchet hanging over all our heads, if we screwed up here.

If a pilot creased or pranged a Spit on Malta (through his own doing, not in enemy action), his punishment was an immediate posting to Kittyhawks (P40's) in the African desert, a sure death, for the P40 was in no way a match for the ME 109 E or F.

It was only the next day that I told someone, Hal Knight, what had happened back there. He said, "The next time, Jerry, call me and I will be there."

Later on, Hal Knight told me that the Luftwaffe Quartermaster General's loss records indicated that three JU 52's of KG.z.b.V. S-11[1] based at Brindisi, Sicily were destroyed on 28 November 1942 by fighter action.

Surely these were the JU 52's heading east for Brindisi that I intercepted. It must then follow that they were indeed two of the JU 52's that I hit quite badly. They cruise ever so slowly and are extremely easy to overtake or toy with and are a bloody big target to fire at. If they were escorted in any way, I saw no other aircraft.

Until quite recently I didn't know what disturbed this character Thompson, our CO in 1942. I have since learned that just prior to my arrival, a F/L Glazebrook, a Canadian from 229 Squadron, Takali, was airborne to engage a reported 50 plus Nazi fighters who were approaching Malta island. 185 Squadron were already engaged with some of the enemy. Some 109's attacked Glazebrook, who fired back. Still in attack mode, he mistook his target and actually shot down Thompson, who crashlanded at Hal Far unhurt.

Colonials were not appreciated by several British types, and because of this incident with the Canadian Glazebrook, my breaking off to engage the 52's surely riled the CO's hair.

His resentment stayed in his craw for years. Even when I was on an RCAF-RAF exchange posting evaluating jets in the UK after the war, he, as CO there, did his best to discredit me. The AOC came to my aid and assessed it as a "clash of personalities."

A sport which all pilots enjoyed on the island was to be able to have a .38 pistol and to pretty well shoot at will. This sport, of course, carried on into the mess and quarters until at one time it wasn't odd to have pilot after pilot shooting behind over his head in sport as something to do.

---

[1] German unit. *Kampfgeschwader zur besonderen Verwendung.* (Battle Group for Special Duties/Transport Group)

On one occasion I was rooming with Rastus Sinclair. Old Sinc never appreciated the small long-tailed lizards that plagued the island. They are harmless creatures and it is not uncommon to see them in the quarters, the mess hall or in homes. Each afternoon, after an early A.M. detail, we would rest. Our beds were covered with a large shawl-type mosquito netting secured at the ceiling then flowing down over the entire bed. I hooked up a string to Sinclair's netting and ran it along the wall over to my side of the room.

As we entered the room I told Sinc that I had seen a bloody lizard in the room that day. He immediately took his .38 pistol and put it beside the pillow. As we lay down, I grabbed the string and gave a jerk. Sinc jumped horizontally and sat bolt upright. Of course, seeing me lying in my bed undisturbed, he said, "Rotten bastard lizards," and began to search for it.

I saw him nearing the string and I departed from my bed but *quick*, Sinc in close pursuit.

I thought I'd fool him and doubled-back into our room. He guessed my move and trapped me as I entered the room. He fired his gun almost point blank as I ducked to the floor. The bullet barely missed my head and lodged itself into the wall, just below a mounted goat's head that I had acquired and hung as a decoration.

In the summer of 1974 I revisited Malta and this house. The building is now a bank, and the manager was most surprised when I asked him if I could inspect the wall of my old bedroom. He possibly thought I was planning a robbery, because he did not let me look.

December 6, 1942 Red Walker, Twitch Bollen, John Houlton and myself were flying low level, Walker leading, just above the water, when Twitch Bollen screamed: "Break port, Jerry!"

I stood on the rudder and pulled as hard as I could. The old Spit was juddering madly. Looking back I could see the bullet splashes just inside and below me. I pulled through a 360-degree turn, gaining height, and rolled inverted to see that Twitch was shooting the hell out of a Hurricane. This poor chap had mistaken us for ME 109s and attacked.

At the dispersal I thanked Twitch for saving me, however, he was not feeling well about the whole episode.

My first encounter with the ME 109 had been on a scramble shortly after my arrival on the island, when Ken Charney, the Flight Commander, claimed one while I was busy trying to hold on. I thought it to be a good aircraft, the 109, as it was handled very well in the melee, a thought which stayed with me throughout. In all other encounters I really was not assessing the 109 but assessing the maneuvers and tactics used in that particular encounter by that particular pilot.

46 / *A Knave Among Knights in their Spitfires*

Jerry with Johnny Miller who was shot down, baled out but was straffed in his dinghy and killed, (Halfar, Malta, 1942).

Goudy Goodwin, Malta, 1942

Mush Sharon, U. K. 1943

Generally in Malta we were in Spit V's against the ME 109E, which was much inferior, but soon the 109F appeared in mixed formations and it was much better. Later on the 109G was about, and, although there were very very few of them, it was much superior to our clapped out Mk V's.

Usually the attacks I made were in turns or from a dive then pulling up into the 109's.

During a melee one is turning wildly, changing direction, mostly alone, and searching in all directions —*Where the hell are they?* They simply disappeared as quick as they were sighted, diving for home.

I did not know of any specs on the 109, the 190, the Macci, the Reggiane, etc. All I knew was what the Spit could do. In later years historians would always try to assess that difference. I knew the silhouette of the enemy and that was all. No one instructed us on dive bombing or any other tactics. My main objective was to engage the enemy in any manner, not to evaluate him. Aircraft recognitions was given only to identify. The knowledge put out on comparisons was to follow in years later.

The quickness of the air battle always surprised one, especially when bounced unexpectedly. To fight a dogfight for three or four minutes would be a lifetime.

I was quite sure in December '42 that I shouldn't see the end of '43, and, enjoying the scene, flew with abandon — for even today at 73 years of age my eyesight is still 20/20, which to me was as good as a Number Two. When I was shot down it was because the odds were against me, not because I didn't see them. Perhaps that outlook was the saviour?

So it was on December 8, 1942. The weather was quite hot and very very hazy indeed, the sea blending with the sky. One could experience vertigo easily.

The plot of eight to ten plus was given. As Jeff Guy (who had been airborne earlier) spotted a JU 88 off Filfla Isle and was giving chase, he fired a call to say he had gotten the bastard. We heard no further R/T from him. The JU was reported to fade from the radar screen just north of Malta. Jeff was never seen again. Nor was the 88.

From the haze above we were bounced by four 109's. A great hassle followed, with everyone split up to fight alone. Things looked OK until I was bounced close in by two 109's, a third closing in from the opposite, astern. He fired striking my engine. There was a great bang, smoke and fire. Time to go.

I immediately pulled hard, jettisoned everything and went over the side. To invert then bale-out, the nose could drop and hold you to the aircraft; it was not a good method.

There was no one around on my way down. It was all quiet as hell.

A few feet above the water I released the chute harness, this being the best procedure not to become tangled in the shrouds.

My dinghy inflated OK and I was picked up by an Air/Sea launch about thirty minutes after. The Air/Sea Rescue was always A1. No great injuries except to my pride.

About that time we were given bombs to put under our wings to dive onto targets in Sicily, Linosa, and Lampedusa. My first trip with the underwing bombs was on the 31st of December, and the feeling that I would never see the 1st of January '43 was very strong. I did everything I could stay off this trip, tried to start the Spit with the switches off — said my oil pressure was low. This was all corrected of course by my Erk, until I finally said, "OK, stand back. Let me the hell out of here."

The trip was most uneventful.

On the first of January, 1943 the CO told me that I could now wear a "crown" along with my sergeant's stripes, (F/Sgt.) as I was leading sections and should wear a little higher rank.

Most of the activity in January '43 consisted of sweeps to Linosa and Sicily, a couple of scrambles, and a search for a Swordfish pilot. In general the retreating 109's in Sicily were just out of reach.

On the 25th we were over Sicily at 27,000 feet, two sections of four Spitfires, when we spotted twelve ME 109's who split up and began to stay just out of range. We tried to turn into them a few times, but they avoided any hassle. We continued to ease our way towards the coast and homeward, and to our surprise, the 109's simply turned northwest towards Palermo, not wanting any part of a fight that day.

On the morning of 15 February, 1943, I rolled over and glanced out of my open window into the most lovely sky I had seen for quite some time and ideal for a lovely sweep. I grabbed one of my flying boots and heaved it at Johnny Miller, my roommate. He rolled over, uttered a bit a blasphemy, and proceeded to get mobile. We arrived at the dispersal some 25 minutes later and began readying our crates. I had talked to the F/Cmdr, and he was to take Red Section and I was to have Green. Green would include MacRae, an Aussie; Johnny Maffre and good old Johnny Miller, all sergeants. We were to do a dive bomber's show on some warehouses in Sicily, approximately twenty miles inland. The show was to come off in approximately one hour. The F/Cmdr called 126 Squadron (Luqa aerodrome). We were to take off together thus giving us a stronger force. We would have eight aircraft and they would have eight.

I strolled over to the Intelligence Room to check over the happenings of the night fighters of the previous night, saw nothing of interest and strolled back toward the dispersal. I was stopped by a Maltese called "Manuel" who tried to sell me an old, old-fashioned Colt (I don't think it would even fire). Getting quite cheesed off with the conversation, I took out my small (Italian) automatic and aimed it at him. He got quite scared (as were all Maltese during those times), and he started to turn towards the dispersal, so I fired a couple of rounds into the sky. My Jesus, the change of pace was terrific.

I looked around and found that I had strolled near the post office, so I decided to send a wire home to Shirley Anne, my sister. I liked this idea, as writing was a great bother and a wire only cost two and six (50 cents). Having completed this task I wandered back to the dispersal, twenty minutes being left before we pushed tits. On entering the room I was greeted by the Winco and he started lecturing me on firing at people and thought perhaps he would have to take our guns away from us. I was brassed off with this as we were going to fly in approximately 20 minutes, so why the hell couldn't he leave us alone?

Finally airborne and starting our long climb towards Sicily, we joined up with the other Spits on the way. Upon our reaching our target, our ground control (Gonda) said they didn't detect any enemy aircraft airborne. It had all the possibilities of a dull show. We approached our target from up-sun and readied ourselves for attack. The other squadron went down first, followed by the F/Cmdr and then our lads. I had slipped out and positioned myself up and well out from the section. They started their dive and I continued on for a few seconds, then rolled over and went straight down. Ahead of me was a black cloud — or wall — of Ack Ack. I knew I had to go through it, so I jammed on full throttle and went screaming for the earth. About 1000 yards ahead of me was another Spit going like a streamlined sack of shit, not attempting a pullout. I glanced at my altimeter — it read 8000 feet — and I was having a hell of a lot of difficulty holding my dive. The pressure builds up terrifically on the control column. Seeing that I couldn't drop my bombs on my target, I spiralled a bit and released my two 250-lb bombs on the corner of a quiet little village, opening up with my cannons at the same time and immediately started my pullout.

I noticed the Spit off to my port strike the ground followed by a brilliant explosion. I don't know what happened to him, probably hit by flak and lost control. I found out later it was a chap I'd trained with in Canada, called Goodyear, his home Newfoundland.

Completing my dive I levelled off at 200 feet and, well behind the other guys, I throttled right back and began hedgehopping towards home.

As I neared the coast, the other Spits were approximately two and a half miles ahead of me and already crossing the south coast of Sicily. At this point I noticed splashes in the water behind and around the boys and realized it was the costal defence opening fire. I scanned the coastline and picked out several pillboxes and several Italian troops — behind our Spits but still in front of me.

I pushed my gun button and gave them cannon and machine gun bullets, at the same time pushing my left then my right rudder, and literally sprayed the coastline. Bodies fell all around; some I could unmistakably see being bowled over by shell fire. I zig-zagged quite quickly and tooled way off to the left of the track home.

I then spotted a submarine on the surface and I pointed the nose in that direction. I opened my motor full, knowing the sub would submerge when he saw me. I dove, and, at approximately 300 feet, I opened fire. His return fire was early and inaccurate. I could see tracer bullets coming toward me. They appeared to come in a long slow pattern, then all at once Zip! they would pass. My bullets struck directly in the conning tower of the sub. I saw one sailor blown off the deck and into the sea as I went zooming across the sub very low. And I kept very low for a considerable distance, out of his firing range. I then climbed and banked for another attack. My speed was less this time, so I started firing at approximately 600 yards away, hoping to screw things up and disorganize the crew a bit. I stopped firing for a moment, and took good aim. At about 850 feet away I opened up again and saw something explode within the tower.

Climbing away I looked over my shoulder and saw the smoking craft. I proceeded home as my gas supply wasn't too good. Also, the boys were no longer around.

Claim nil. No witnesses.

I arrived over Hal Far, called for permission to land, banking sharply, already slipping in for my touchdown. I taxied to my pen and my Erks guided me around into position for parking. My rigger, seeking that I'd fired, hopped onto my wing with a big smile and said, "What'd you get, Jerry?" (Bloody good rigger, same age as myself).

My reply was, "One church, a pill box, couple of Eyteis I know of, and I hope that Jesus sub burst. Make it three Eyties; I blew one off the sub."

He immediately said, "What? No aircraft?"

Snarling (Jesus, I could have filled him in!), I said, "Can't knock down what we don't find, and those yellow dogs are sure staying away. I'll get a cow for you the next time I'm over, OK?"

He said, "Isn't any good to me. Can't get it anyway."

"Well, I'll get one any how," I promised. I then tooled off into the dispersal, where the chaps were already discussing the show. The Christly Winco came over and proceeded to renew the balling-out for firing at Manuel. Nothing more for me to say, I thought.

We had no other activity that morning, only to call Ops and find who went into the deck (this being Goodyear). A bit of standby was carried out in case the Hun came over. He didn't.

We were relieved at 12:30 by A Flight. Manuel drove us to our billets. He later became a very good friend of mine. Even gave me the old Colt.

The first of March we were again over Sicily when we were bounced by four N4E 109's. During this melee, old Johnny Miller received a hit in his motor and he had to bale out. His parachute opened in order, but he had some difficulty opening his inflatable rubber dinghy. The Hun at this point had pulled out of the area, so I kept circling Miller. Realizing his situation, I undid my parachute and harness and snapped off my dinghy, opened my hood and threw my dinghy to him in the water. He was not able to open mine either. Withy threw him his as well. Johnny was picked up, water-logged some hours later, by the Walrus flying boat and we found out that he simply forgot to pull the safety pin on the C02 bottles. (Dumb screw!)

On returning to base I refuelled and was immediately scrambled with Knight to act as top cover for a pilot in a dinghy seven miles off Sicily. The rescue launch picked him up OK and we returned to Hal Far job completed.

One week later, Johnny Miller was shot down again. This time he got into his floating dinghy but he was strafed in his rubber boat by the Germans and was killed (riddled to pieces by Germans).

One aid that all pilots carried with them was a scramble card. This card was circular and divided into 8 sections. Each section was named for a different area of the islands. In the center was a smaller circle; it too had 8 sections, each having a different letter and an altitude.

The reason for this card was that the enemy radio would give us false height or angles or places to patrol or scramble to. Each day the position of the key letter "O" for ORANGE would be changed by our operations, thereby causing a failure in the enemy's deception. For example, instructions for 14 February would possibly be "Gozo." So on the 14th, rotate "O" to Gozo, and when directed to the Hun: Angels "Z", Patrol "A", you would climb to 25,000 feet over Grande Harbour.

On the third of March 1943, we were scrambled as Green section to intercept a plot of ten-plus German planes. I was leading with Mercer, Al Laing and Mac MacLaren.

We were climbing at 160 mph until we reached 16,000 feet and then I increased our climbing speed to 175 mph for battle purposes, heading due north until Gonda control reported to me that the little jobs were going south and were approaching Grande Harbour, Malta, and that there were approximately twelve-plus. Our position at this time was farther West. George Mercer, my Number 2, was flying on my right. Al Laing was Number Three, and Mac MacLaren my Number 4 (Al's Number 2). His position was on my left. We had made a cross-over 90 degree turn and were going east now. I increased my oxygen flow to the required at 18,000 feet, a height that we had just reached when I noticed my radio button had snapped out. This I corrected.

Off to my right and below I could see two Spits — the CO, S/Ldr Joe Crafts, and the F/Cmdr F/L Withy who had also scrambled and were joining the show. My section was the highest and the only one close to the Hun.

At this point the Ack Ack had just fired two pointer rounds for us at the Hun. Simultaneously I spotted two ME 109's 3000 feet above and at one o'clock. I disregarded them for the moment and also picked up three more 2000 feet above and at five o'clock. I called Al in my section and I asked if he could see them, and told him to keep an eye on them. He was on the blower saying, "OK, Jerry."

At this point the CO and Withy (CO leading, I presume) had crossed beneath us and were going slightly Northeast from us — and from the Hun.

The CO called me and said to join them, which I considered quite ridiculous at the time, being right in the center and below the Hun, so I made a flat turn to the left of 20 degrees, which left the sun about 4 o'clock to us and not a very smart position.

The two Huns by now had crossed directly above us and were at about nine o'clock to me. The other three Huns were about seven o'clock, still 2000 feet about above. Lovely position for them, I thought. My radio button flicked out again at this point and the Huns, two of them, were diving and attacking us.

I waited for a few seconds until both Jerries opened fire at George Mercer and myself. I had seen five or six explosive shells burst behind me and well out of range, then I screamed, "Break port, Green Section!" and simultaneously turned to port as viciously as possible, avoiding all contact with the enemies' bullets.

My section kind of went for shit at this point.

Al Laing and MacLaren, my 3 and 4 (Mac incidently didn't see a damned thing), broke right, passing Christly close to me. George Mercer, the mad dog, probably weighing up the others, didn't break quite fast enough and received quite a packet. He was clobbered to hell. (We would find later that his wings were full of holes, his

52 / *A Knave Among Knights in their Spitfires*

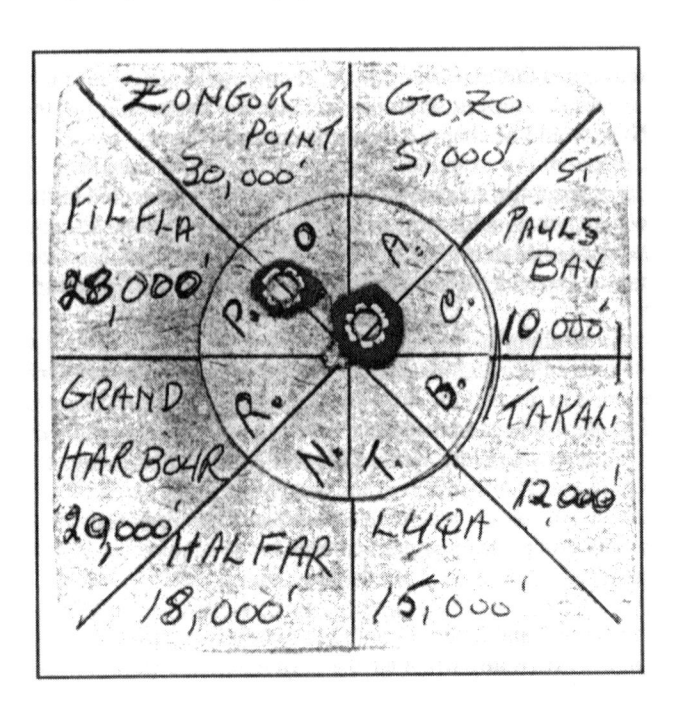

A Malta " Scramble Card ", with the key letter " O ".
Each day it was changed to confuse the enemy when pilott directed to fly.
i.e. " R " - Angels - " N ".

"My Relief—I hope?"

A Cartoon of the time.

undercarriage would not go down, and his engine cowling had been blown off.) He crash landed at base after breaking — spiraling all the way — for home.

Al and Mac in breaking had been left about 2000 feet lower than myself. Heading south towards Malta now I waggled my wings in a vain effort to make them rejoin formation, calling on the R/T, "OK you guys, let's join up here." George had already turfed off homeward.

I damned well don't blame him.

To my left, 800 yards above and going across me at 10 o'clock were two 109's. On my right were two more flying in the same line as me, only about 900 yards above. Directly behind me were two more, bloody near attacking.

I waited for their move — which damned well comes quick — and the two behind dove to attack.

First a hesitation, then, jamming my pitch and throttle full, I broke to the right, seeing tracers and cannon shell pass well over my head

Avoiding the attack I climbed violently for a vantage spot, but the two Huns on my right made a tight turn to port, keeping themselves in a very advanced spot and well above. The other two Huns which had crossed above on my left also made a left turn to sort of box me in momentarily. One of the other Huns who had first attacked, being foxy, attacked me again from astern. I then broke hard starboard, balls out and climbing bastardly hard for a 360-degree turn.

The Hun obviously turned a bit but I found myself in the advantage at this point, with the Hun ahead of me, slightly to the right and 500 feet above, approximately 750 year away. (Bloody good!) I checked the air above me and saw the other two going away and in the opposite direction, and the fool that attacked me looked as if he was going straight up and well forward to me.

I closed to attack the two in front of me, fired at one, saw strikes at the wing root area, then fired at the second 109 and saw strikes in the tail section. Just as I was about to blow the Hun to eternity, the other bitch attacked me from very close up. Cannon and machine gun bullets tore through my aircraft, blowing large holes in my wings, exploding my motor and ruining my controls. Glycol or gas, probably both and oil as well, drenched my face and body. I could taste glycol. I reached for my goggles, only to find they had just been torn from my helmet by a passing bullet. Bullets began rattling against my backbone, and was saved only by my Spit's armour plating. I tried desperately to wiggle my ass forward a few more inches but in vain. Seconds more and shells plowed through the door of my cockpit — missing my left arm, which invariably lay on the throttle quadrant — smashing my instrument panel. A bullet also tore across my left sleeve and glove, exposing my bare hand.

My damned machine was completely out of control. Old J.C. was now taking over. My throttle and controls had no response. I fought desperately but was thrown around like a ball. I felt for my straps and pulled them as best I could, which didn't help at all. The only music I had was the continued hail of bullets from the Huns (which I could hear) of the victorious enemy. He must have felt good. I would have.

I was pushed down and forward now into the cockpit, unable to sit straight and damned near blinded, only able to see occasionally directly at my feet.

I cursed aloud madly, more like a maniac now. I envisioned, and could actually feel inwardly a crash into the sea, my body striking the already battered instrument panel. Scared to death, I shook my head and fought like a bastard, rubbed my eyes and caught a flickering glimpse of my airspeed, which was well past the 500 mark. Blinded again, I felt as though I was in a spin, but at that speed it could only be a fast tight, spiral downward. I immediately corrected for a dive which felt to the left, and abandoned all hope now of regaining control of this crate (which I loved admirably, being the fastest machine, I thought, on our squadron), and tried to bale out, only to find that I couldn't move due to G forces in the vicious steep descending spiral. I had pulled the pin from my harness strap but left my helmet on, hoping to hear Christ-knows-what from my already demolished radio. My canopy was already open. I had opened it during the climb towards the enemy, as we often flew without them, enabling us to see better, for sand was deteriorating the perspex and the supply of them was limited anyway. The canopy sticks out a further two inches or so, and it could catch one's chute when baling out. Better to be rid of it. I could have jettisoned it, although a test on the ground proved they were jamming using this method, which only meant a pilot in that condition was trapped to die a lonely and dishonest death.

However, still blinded, I fought frantically to gain my feet, but was still unable to move. The most deadly smell I have yet to taste drifted up past my nose. I placed my hands behind my knees, and pulled them up until they rested with my hands behind the control column. Taking a deep breath I pushed with a last vain effort and the most un-Godly experience I've ever had until that moment happened — the aircraft seemed to shake violently and sounded like a pail of stones had been fling at it. My head was jerked back and a noise similar to a champagne bottle being opened sounded. A great rush of air and I couldn't hear or feel a damned thing more.

I'd swear to Christ my right arm was torn off. I tried to see it and, with the sense of my arm, bring it into view, without success.

My position: I was tumbling in space at an altitude of approximately 17,000 feet from earth — only I was directly over the gorgeous Mediterranean. On my left small finger I wore a ring, which I was quite fond of, and I was trying to see if I had lost it. I found later that what I felt was the coolness on my hand when my glove was blown off.

I suppose I got scared again, for I suddenly reached for the rip cord of my parachute and gave a thorough yank. So complete and smooth was this motion that, though normally a pilot returns with his ring-grip, mine just vanished with the pull, into the Heavens. I was instantly pulled erect and my Jesus neck felt as if Joe Blow had hammered me. I couldn't look upwards, which maddened me. The boys always spoke of how lovely a canopy of a chute looked fully plumed while in a descent. Out of the corner of my left eye I could swear I could see my neck. It had swollen from the jerk of my helmet which had been torn off my head in the cockpit escape.

I also felt a tingling sensation in both my legs, the position of which I could not detect. Swaying a bit with the breezes or the momentum (guess I'll never know which), I found I was gasping for air. It felt as if I had been running for blocks. I realized afterwards it was due to the lack of oxygen at my unknown height.

To my left, far in the distance I could see Mount Etna, Italy, and her snowcapped peak. The shores of Sicily were quite noticeable and becoming. On my right, approximately 20 miles away, lay my goal, Malta, which looked bloody good, but then I glanced downward to nothing but sea. The waves looked quite violent; whitecaps were visible as far as the eye could see, and I, not able to swim a damned stroke, hadn't a clue in the world what to do when I would most certainly drop below the surface.

I immediately felt my Mae West, patted it and pulled the CO2 (carbon dioxide) bottle release. It blew up perfectly. I smiled a bit and began preparing my dinghy for inflation, unsnapping the snaps and pulling it half out.

I should note that the situation of this article is beneath one's pants; a pilot sits on the dingy, as it is mounted on top of his parachute.

After exposing as much as I dared of the dingy, I removed the glove from my right hand, looked it over, and threw it away. The damned thing went up instead of down. I then began removing my flying boots. THIS HURT. I had just acquired them. Their previous owner had been a chap named Sgt. Carmody who had been shot down a week before and had disappeared completely. They were lovely boots, comfortable as slippers and they shone like patent leather "glossy black." I removed one boot, held it out at arm's length, and dropped it. The damned thing went so far down it disappeared. I never did see it hit the water.

I tried to remember a few things a pal of mine had done two days earlier in baling out. That was good old Johnny Miller, who now holds an office in hell, I'm sure. He had removed his pants, but I abandoned this idea. He had done this in the water, and I still had my chute on.

I just waited, checked my time — by my watch 11:23 A.M. — tried to swing myself toward Malta but gave this up as the swinging became too violent.

Off and down in the distance I had a fleeting glimpse of my Spitfire crashing into the sea with a lovely trail of smoke left behind her. 'Bloody good crate, that! Billing.'

I caught a glimpse of two aircraft directly over Malta but lost them in the glare of the sun.

This was the most wonderful and enjoyable trip I'll ever have, so I thought— not a sound and not a thing around. To think I don't want Heaven but I had just finished trying to go.

After dropping my last boot at 50 feet, I set myself for the great plunge. I was about 15 feet from the water when I snapped the release control of my chute. I dropped beneath the surface and then grabbed my nose to hold my breath (a little late).

The feeling I had under water was that I kept going down, down, down, then everything went light. Surfacing, I opened my eyes. Waves approximately 25 feet in height were all around me.

I got my dinghy out. It was held to me by a dog leash attached to my Mae West. I hauled it toward me and started inflating it. At this point my legs became tangled in the chute cords. This terrified me very much, as chaps quite often drown this way, especially non-swimmers. Luckily my dinghy blew up perfectly — only upside-down. I placed both hands on its side, and it turned over quite easily. In fact it amazed me how easily it righted itself. I pulled the dinghy towards me and drew it beneath me without trouble. I then began to bale the bloody water out. The chute and supplies began to sink, so I was forced to cut them loose.

At this point there came the most Christly roar I've ever heard, a gust of wind, a zoom, and an aircraft passing Jeezly close to me. I thought I'd had it. But it was a Spitfire. He pulled straight up and chased two 109's away from me. I'm sure they had been about to attack.

After the 109's left, my rescuer, having arriving just in time, came tearing down on me again and scared the living stuff right out of me. Goody and Steve, who I found out later was the mad dog, then resumed normal patrol with the others above until the rescue launch approached and threw a rope to me.

Climbing aboard, I asked if I could speak to the chaps above on the R/T. They handed me a microphone. I gave Goody a short blast for which I'm today I'm sorry. He then really began to beat up the boat. The crew were not pleased.

The crew took me below and they stripped me of my clothing. They then wrapped me in blankets, dressed my wounds, and gave my neck a thorough massage, and left me lying on the floor of the boat. The only worry I had was: 'Where were my watch and my small automatic?' Once I had these back in my possession, I immediately asked for my drink of rum, which is given to all pilots picked out of the drink if they are able to take it. They handed me a tumbler full of good old navy style rum. I smacked my lips and lifted the glass. Hold Christ, strong! The bloody stuff came right back up. I handed back the remains of the tot, rolled over and shivered the rest of the way to Malta.

Claims nil, as I had been left alone with the Hun and had no cine film and no witness.

The next morning I felt terrible. I could not move my arms or legs because of the soreness, and my neck was paining violently. On the front of my left leg was a hole the size of a thin pencil straight to the bone, but it never bled. I taped it over and it healed okay. The front of my right leg was scraped or gorged with an open wound of six inches long and three inches wide — terribly sore and festering. The MO put a taped bandage over it that about drove me wild. I approached him and he said, "I have some 'new skin' that I can paint on to protect it."

Well, when that dried I was in real pain, as the hardened stuff pulled, and the throbbing caused me to start peeling this mess off the wound. Had I had the medic within my sight I would have shot him. It was unbearable. I peeled every piece off with my fingernails. At the time I could hardly see, because of the tears in my eyes, but the relief was worth it.

For my wounds I was given one week's rest and a Hurricane to fly to Tripoli. Old Knight was to accompany me.

On arriving at Costel Benito aerodrome just outside of Tripoli, Knight called me over and gestured to where a Lodestar was readying to take off, "Let us ask the old chap over there if he is going to Cairo. Maybe we can hitch a ride."

I agreed, having no idea how far Cairo was.

The pilot was an old pukka type AVM — switch and all — named Saule. "Of course, lads," he said. "Hop in. We are leaving very shortly."

Hours later we were still heading east having made brief stops at Benghazi, Tobruk, Marble Arch, El Alamein, and Alexandria. Old Saule gave us oranges to eat and acted a very fine host. Little did he know how I was becoming concerned about our return trip. Hell, I was supposed to be resting in Tripoli. I moved close to Knight who was a F/L: against my F/Sgt and said, "How are we going to get back?"

He replied, "I really do not care. If necessary I will head south and go home." Knight was from South Africa.

Right there I made an immediate decision and said, "I am going with you."

As soon as we landed my first task was to get rid of my rank. Knight gave me one of his rank badges, and for the next 10 days I impersonated an officer.

I took a 2-day trip down the Nile, and found that most interesting. Our 7-day leave quickly lapsed and my money was low. I visited the RAF accounts section in Cairo, and they gave me 10 pounds on my paybook. I never did repay that advance.

On the 11th day Knight came up with the brilliant idea that we should go straight to AVM Broadhurst, a mean old codger, and tell him our story. Perhaps he would help us. I stuck my sergeant's stripes on with some gum, and we were both marched into his office. I might say that he was most unpleasant. In fact, he was damned upset when he heard our request. But he said, "I will tell you what I will do. I will give you each a Kittyhawk to deliver to the Mareth line, and by God, you had better not prang them."

This was my first trip in the machine that we all dreaded. If any Spitfire pilot pulled a boner or was assessed as below average, he was posted to a Kittyhawk squadron as a reprimand, or to an easier type aircraft. Freddie Vance had that happen to him from our Malta squadron.

The trip across the desert was hot, but uneventful. Then we hitched a ride back to Malta on an old Dakota on the supply route out of Tripoli.

On arriving back on the squadron we both told W/C Peter prosser Hanks what we had done. His comment was, "Bloody good show, chaps. I would have liked to have been there."

While we were gone, on the 8th of March, F-L Withy was shot down in the aircraft I had flown off the carrier. Johnny Miller was also shot down while circling Withy. Johnny baled out only to be shot dead in his dinghy by 109's.

I guess most everyone who ever flew on the island in those days was shot down at one time or another. If you were fortunate not to be directly in the bullets' path when they struck all round you, you survived. It must be true to say that the armour plating or the engine or the one and a half inch thick windscreen allowed many pilots to escape and not head west. It is frightening to see your wings being torn to hell by the bullets of an enemy shooting you down and you just cannot get out of the situation.

On March 21st we were scrambled to intercept a plot of 12 plus, but never came closer than 5 miles to the 109's as they turned and headed home. The month of April was devoted mainly to dive bombing Sicily or Lampedusa, or nightly single attacks on the target of your choice in Sicily. Fighter interceptors were now beginning to be less.

On the 5th of May I lead a section of four to intercept a plot of 60 plus. I had just begun to enter the fray when my engine gave a loud bang and my oil pressure dropped very low.

I half rolled and went screaming for home to find that something in my supercharger had failed, causing the muffled explosion.

Out of this same attack one brand new ME 109G was shot down and force landed fully intact at Luqa aerodrome to be studied by the boffins, confirming that the 109G's were about. The types were made in the U.S.A.

On the 8th of May, Dink Nesbitt and I were scrambled to intercept a JU 88 south of Filfla. There were too many clouds around.

My last trip on the island was on the 9th of May. Again we were scrambled to intercept a plot of 8 plus. We sighted four 109's, but they disappeared in the clouds as they had the day before.

I left the island on the 19th of May, 1943 in a bloody old DC3 aircraft, very unhappy to be leaving, but glad I had surpassed the lifespan of 2 to 3 months estimated for a fighter pilot in Malta. The trip was uneventful, but you might imagine the anxiety and anticipation we all had, when our memories were alive with the Liberator prang and the drowning of the pilots before us in November. Leaving with me were Goody, Dean Kelly, and Mush Sharon, bound for Gibraltar for a week to wait for a boat to transport us to the U.K.

I had lost many friends by then, both in the U.K. and on the island — Byrd and Brown killed at the OTU; Rene, Jackal, and Henderson no longer around from 19 Squadron; nor were Peters or Carter who had been shot down over Malta. Carmody, Guy, Miller, Parks, MacRae all were shot down. Mutch and Heatherington were killed in the Liberator prang.

Goody was still with me. Of course he was at it again and shot the hell out of everything with his .38. Our quarters in Gibraltar, which were Nissen huts, were pockmarked, and you could see the stars above at night. What a buddy.

Old Goody had been up for his commission on several occasions. At Malta once he was told: 'Okay, you will get it.' But at lunch later in the mess, as the W/C reached out to retrieve the one remaining slice of bread on the plate, Goody grabbed his fork, speared the slice, dragged it to him and said, "Get your bloody hooks off that. That's mine."

Yes, his commission was deferred.

On another occasion Goody was in the town of Rabat and, having a touch of Ambeet wine in this veins, spotted a fair maiden. With a cup of Ambeet in his hands, Goody took off after her. Well, the local populace saved the fair maiden. Goody was put on the waiting list again.

He was a terrible man, a real heller, whom I found plaguing my career from start to finish. I am rather indebted to this character though, as he saved my life from the Hun and the sea.

I had spoken to Goody shortly after my bale-out, and he of course lectured me: "Keep you arse clear and look around you once in a while, you clot."

A very short time later, some sloppy individual forgot the rules and allowed his tail to become dirtied, ending up in the Mediterranean, shot to hell. I was scrambled to search for the dinghy, and found the little runt — he wasn't in his bloody dinghy, but was trying his best to stay afloat in this tattered Mae West — thus returning my debt for that period.

Finally a troop transport, the *California*, arrived at Gibraltar. (The *California*, I am told, was sunk by the German U boats on its next trip out.)

We were loaded aboard on 16 May for 6 days ocean voyage to Britain.

I have never really appreciated a boat, especially on the high seas where one can see the entire ship in a half a day. To spend a week or so on a troop ship is beyond anyone's imagination.

The Eyties had turned in 1943, but there remained multi Eyties who were strongly loyal to Mussolini. On board this ship were several hundred prisoners of war being taken to the UK. These prisoners were confined in a fenced-in area on the entrance to their quarters or complete deck (the first deck below the main deck).

We sergeants were given quarters in the hold of the ship, even after completing our first tour of operations against the enemy. We were treated badly.

The ship was overcrowded and the stench unbearable once one left the open air on the deck. We were given hammocks to swing in the hold, two decks below the prisoners. The bloody floor in the hold was always awash with water that swayed and swirled from side to side with the rolling of the ship. Some of the chaps washed their socks, and those hung about front the pipes over our hammocks, only half clean to add to the smell.

"Mush" Sharon, an ex-Wardair or Max Ward pilot, gagged at the smell, so much that he never went below. He took his hammock out on deck, and lashed himself to the ship at night to ensure he would not wash overboard. He slept in the cold and rain every night of the whole trip.

For the rest of us to leave the hold for air or to eat, we were obliged to walk past the scruffy, smelly Eyties. They knew where we had been flying and would spit at us each time we passed their area, and use abusive language in their mother tongue. I had never been really impressed with the Italian code of ethics.

The food was always a hash type of mush, bread, and dishwater tea. We would make sure we were at the purser's office at opening to buy any type of chocolate or whatever. It was mostly 'whatever', at a very high price. My weight after leaving Malta was 138 - 142 pounds, so it never really required too much to fill that shrunken stomach.

An interesting statistic to note is the number of "Colonials" who fought in the skies over Malta during that period. Canadians, New Zealanders, Australians, South Africans, Rhodesians, etc., proved to be over 80 percent. I suppose it was easier to send this type of pilot out of England, rather than send the pilots from home.

****

When 11 June, 1940 saw Italy declare war against the allies, the headline in *The Malta Times* read: "Mussolini's Cowardly Act." One of the first places the Eyties bombed on Malta was the Hal Far aerodrome, the base from which I few in 1942/43. These bomber were S. M. 79's.

Because of these bombings, thousands of Maltese residents left the Grande Harbour area and flocked to the small villages in the southern parts of the island. Malta itself is not self-supporting, and had depended on Italy, mainly Sicily, for food import. During the war no food was coming, and nutritional food was simply not available. What food there was was highly rationed and cooked in the community kitchens in huge round iron pots five feet wide. Each family would visit their kitchen for their daily meal, which was dished out proportionately to each person. I have seen the local people's skin break out in sores from lack of vitamins. I noticed a fair damsel boarding a bus one day; on the calf of her leg was a sore, and when she stopped to board the bus, the muscle tightened, breaking the skin to reveal the festering mess.

Yet the Maltese stood defiant, surrounding by over 1500 miles in all directions by the Nazi and the Eytie. The anti-Eytie campaign flourished, and anything with Eytie flavour was extinguished. Street signs were even changed.

When sirens sounded to warn of the approaching Eytie bombers, the Maltese shunned the air raid shelters in defiance of the police warnings, and rushed to their roof tops to have a grandstand view of the spectacular aerial battles. Mandatory take-cover orders for the populace were passed. However, after the first month of Eytie bombings, these orders were ignored, even though fines were imposed for disobedience. The court became overcrowded and the restrictions were lifted.

Not long afterward, the Luftwaffe also appeared. Wave after wave of Stuka bombers attacked the island. British fighters were scrambled to repel them, but, alas, they were too few to afford any great defense.

The attacks were steady night and day, and by 16 May 1942, over 2000 homes were destroyed in over 370 bombing raids. They attacked Hal Far and the main aerodrome, Luqa. Each day saw over 100 Stuka bombers mixed with JU 88's and S.M. 79's raiding the island. The Luftwaffe drew many squadrons from the Russian front for the first months, but, because of their numbers, the enemy had complete mastery of the skies, running at will over the island.

In March 1942, rumors of the Spitfires' arrival sent great chills amongst the people. Their arrival was greeted with awe, and this new sound over Malta was heard in the ghostly "hissing" and "whistling" in the air above.

The Malta Spitfires now created the most efficient force for its size anywhere in the world. There were simply too many combats during an hour or throughout the day even to attempt to describe them all. Impossible. Many many pilots whom I had known paid with the supreme sacrifice of their lives — to have an official report, a brief note recording the death of a fighter pilot — and then their names were simply forgotten in the heat of battle. I was all in a day's work, at $1.50 a day. These few remarks from the pilots never conveyed the swift destruction and fury and depth of a dogfight.

On 15 August 1942, a large convoy was due to arrive with desperately needed Spitfires and supplies. The aircraft carrier *Eagle* was sunk August 11th, and, with that, the battle in the Mediterranean raged. In this battle two merchant ships and one oil tanker, the *Ohio* sank, but its precious cargo of fuel was salvaged when its wreck was towed into harbour on the 15th. Spitfires gave continuous cover to the ships. They were greatly outnumbered, but destroyed many of the enemy.

Despite these supplies from the convoy, the people of the island were on the verge of starvation. In August and September 1942, a lull in the fighting occurred. My arrival on the island was during the September lull. Then, in October, the German airforce returned to attack. Over 1400 sorties by the Krauts took place with their losses being over 120 plans. The RAF lost only 25 Spitfires.

The last heavy raid on the Maltese Islands occurred 30 July 1943, two months after I left.

King George VI awarded the George Cross for Valour to the Island of Malta to honour the brave people who fought during the Blitz of 1942.

In retrospect, Malta itself is as pleasant a place as anyone would like to live. The temperature remains constant the year round, at about 80 degrees.

The feeling of the soft sea breezes against my skin is one I shall never forget.

I had, and still have, many friends on the island. Mr. Brincat of the Siesta Motel at Meida; Emanuel, the bus driver; and Mrs. Bonicie of Birzebbugga. I often rowed out in Kalafrana Bay in the clear blue water to watch the divers recovering goods from the hold of a merchant ship laying on it side, having been bombed by the enemy.

After the first time I was shot down into the sea, Willy Fursman, our fourteen year-old bartender, came to me and said that his mother wished to have my clothes to wash. God, I thought, I am that dirty! Her reason, however, was to ensure that the salt water was rinsed out of my clothes so they would not rot. Every morning for over two weeks, this woman met me on the street on my trek to the bus to give me a flower. What appreciation!

The isle of Comino, situated between Malta and Gozo, was said to be a haven for kings and rich pirates. The beautiful and richly decorated buildings certainly bear this out. St. Paul's Bay, in the north, was cleared as the most attractive and prominent beach, though I preferred Kalafrana Bay and the small town of Birzebbugga. Other days of idleness found me in the graveyard of aircraft, situated between Qrendi strip and Hal Far. I would examine the remains of enemy and allied aircraft, and from here found out that the JU 88's vulnerable areas were on the starboard side; all pumps and electrical paraphernalia were hooked up there.

Malta today is slowly being recognized by people for its beauty, which I am sure will attract tourists to spoil it forever. These isles, known world wide for their finely worked silver and lace, shall become another Acapulco, sure as hell.

Today Malta is an area of superb retreat, with an air of tranquility, which, once visited and tasted, can never be forgotten. Malta in 1942 was a paradise for fighter pilots. Although dirty and without food, it offered plenty of action.

One strange phenomenon that I remember is a persistent gathering of small clouds above these islands, as if they are topped by some sort of halo. These clouds were visible for miles and excellent for me to navigate by.

I was rather sorry and reluctant to leave Malta, but I had lost considerable weight during my stay, being plagued with "the Dog" endlessly, and I felt that a good meal anywhere would be nice.

The following is a Spitfire acrobatic routine by Mr. Alex Henshaw M.B.E., Chief Test Pilot on most all Spitfires that came off production during World War II. The following is that extract from Henshaw's book *Sigh for a Merlin*. He was asked to demonstrate often for the 'Wheels'. Many were clueless on the Spitfires capabilities. This demonstration was flown by Alex (a treasured friend and an exceptional pilot).

I have never seen anyone flick-roll a Spitfire and I must say that I always found it a little frightening to abuse a machine and have it flash out of your control, if only for a few seconds, like a young spirited blood-horse.

On the pull-out from the flick-roll, sometimes I would open the engine flat out in another vertical climb and at approximately 1200 feet push the nose over forward and with the engine closed complete the half of an outside loop, usually in those days called a 'bunt'. I never liked this manoeuvre either; it was easy but required heavy pressure forward on the control column and you could not afford to misjudge at 1200 feet: with the nose going over down towards the ground the speed built up at such an alarming rate that it left no room to change your mind until it was too late. At the bottom of the inverted dive I would usually 'round off' to a few feet above the ground and then with as much pressure as I dare use on the control column — I say 'dare' because I found it more disconcerting and frightening to 'black-out' from excessive negative 'G' than I did from high loads in the positive position — I would push the machine into an almost vertical climb and then as it lost momentum from the negative 'G' position, pull the control gently over to form a half-loop, hoping as I did that the engine would burst into life as I opened the throttle. This it usually did with a spectacular sheet of flame pluming from the exhaust stubs caused by unused fuel which had accumulated during the inverted manoeuvre. With the engine now on full power I would do a series of very low rolls left and right in front of the audience at below hangar height finishing in the inverted position from which I would 'raise' the undercarriage, pull into a tight, fast engine-off turn and lower the flaps as I touched down for the landing.

63 / Chapter 5

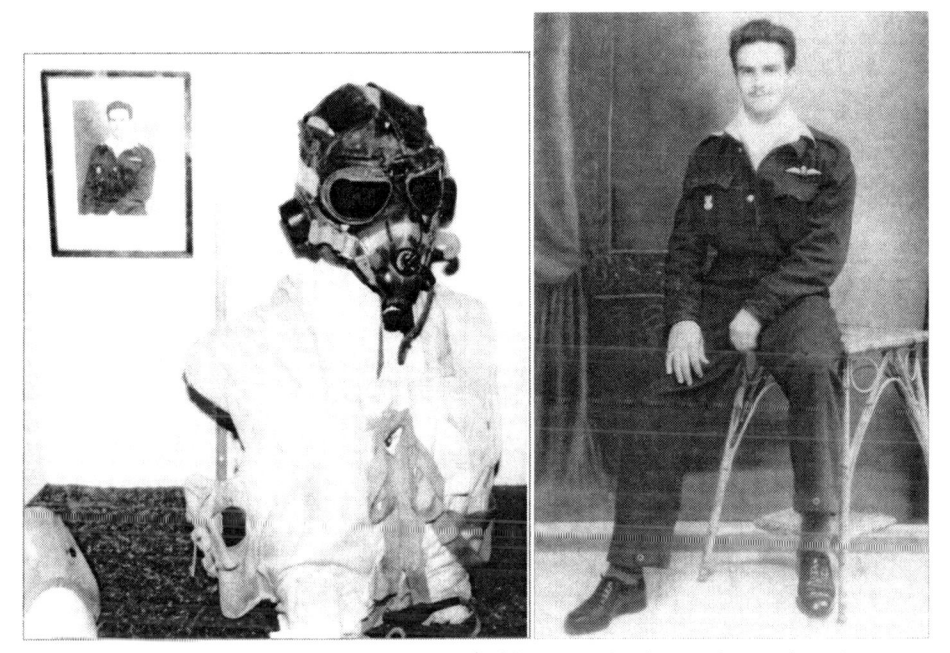

Jerry's flight equipment and photograph. Now on display at the Malta Museum

Enemy plane identification cards issued to Spitfire pilots serving on Malta

6. SPITFIRE O.T.U. INSTRUCTOR
AND ONE MONTH'S LEAVE IN CANADA

I arrived back in the U.K. and, prior to going to a Spitfire Operational Training Unit, I was posted to an instructor school at Kirton Lindsay. This course was on the Miles Master, an aircraft that never really impressed me. The Master I was a dog with an in-line engine — leaked all over the place. Fortunately we had mostly re-engined Master II's and III'S.

Dean Kelly and I invariably flew together as mutual pilots. Old Mush Sharun had a bit of trouble here with his instructor. I guess it was because of Mush's appearance. I always said he looked like a Pollack. He looked like Edward G. Robinson — exactly like — never wore a tunic, a .38 in each boot. He didn't impress our British instructors. He didn't impress them at all. Good man. He didn't make it. Kelly and I each received an above-average assessment and graduated with a "Q" — qualified instructor. With an instructor rating we were then able to take pilots from Canada, who had trained on Harvards, and turn them loose on Hurricanes and Spits.

I often flew inverted and did much gliding and turning while inverted to keep in good form. One day as I rolled to the inverted position, fuel from the tank covered my windscreen (as the fuel tank is immediately in front of the windscreen). I rolled out and landed, then demanded to the F/Sgt maintenance to have brought to me the person responsible for not properly securing the gas top.

Shortly a wee lass entered crying. She said, "It was I who did not tighten the fuel cap, Sir."

"Stop crying", I said. "And forget it. You'd better meet me at the Oswold Pub tonight."

"Oh, yes, Sir. I shall."

Each morning I arrived early before the other chaps to ensure that I would do the air test which involved a complete beat-up of the drome with a good fifteen minutes of low aerobatics. This wee lassie would invariably have the coal stove going in the Nissen hut with a cup of hot tea for me.

Good show.

On another trip, as I was flying inverted I began to smell an electrical short. Looking down and behind my seat, I saw smoke was coming up quite badly. I throttled off and dove for the drome, keeping my cockpit hood shut. I slipped violently and cut off all power. The Spit rolled to a stop. I leaped out, and in minutes the Spit caught fire and burned out completely. No one even shooting.

The cause assessed was that some tool had been left in the radio area, causing a short and the fire. No one confessed to that one.

From instructor school, I went on to Kirton-In-Lindsay, Lincolnshire, in mid-July, 1943, and began instructing pilots on Spitfires the art of dogfighting tactics. Some of the pilots were Jerry Bell, later of 401 Squadron; Bill Waterton, later to be a test pilot at Auro Canada; and S/Ldr Burne, who had a wooden leg. At Kirton I also met Dean Dover, Jimmy Talala, Frank Mason, W/C Berry, J. Neil, and old Steve Randall.

I would get three or four days off and journey to London to see the shows and the sights. We all used to eat at a small restaurant on Denman Street called the S.F. Grill (now gone). Some of the premier players at the Strand or Leicester Square also gathered at the S.F. During the war, the only people who received milk in the restaurant were children, but the waitresses would smuggle milk to us, serving it in a cup to hide this luxury.

I had received my King's Commission as, unbeknownst to me, Steve Randall had made application for me. I was now an officer and a gentleman the rank of Pilot Officer and Flying Officer confirmed. Steve and I visited the restaurant, and to my surprise, they locked the doors and threw a small party to celebrate my commission. Present were some of the players from Leicester Square playing in "Strike a New Note and Strike it Again" —— Zoe Gale, Sid Fields and others —— a great surprise for I had no idea that anyone would notice or even be interested. Steve would recall this episode, I'm sure, for I gained the uniform of a Canadian chap, John Mobray, who had been killed in Malta. He had received his commission just before going to Malta but left it in London.

At the O.T.U., Lorne Cameron and I were involved in gunnery mostly, and it was through Lorne's demand that I ended up on 401 Squadron in early '44. But before that, in mid-January, 1944, I was told that I had one month's leave to Canada. I also held in my hand a signal to report to 401 Squadron. The bloody war is on, and they're going to give me a month leave! I called Cameron, who advised me that I had to take the leave first but to call him immediately when I arrived back in the U.K. to join 401.

The boat passage home was terrible. A troop ship on the North Atlantic in the middle of winter was no place to be, everyone either lined up for food or sick all over the place and hanging over the rails. Our bunks were wooden things nailed together three high in the hold.

Upon reaching land, we rumbled by train across the eastern part of Canada to stop in Ottawa. Here a large crowd waited, and we were greeted with bands and the usual well-wishers. The Accounts section took us aside and gave us our back pay. Old Kelly, Sharun, Red Thompson, Gordon Lapp and I all bulged at our pockets, and to this day I have no idea how much was given.

Red Thompson and I pressed on to Windsor, unannounced, and when I arrived at the factory where my father worked, I tapped him on the back and said, "Hello, Joe."

His jaw dropped and he said, "Well, for Christ's sake." The same type of reception occurred with my mother, only she lay prostrate on the divan, unable to breathe for some time. Guess it was quite a shock, because they had heard that I had been injured somewhat with a possible loss of a leg or two.

The days that followed were hectic. I guess I should have gone across the border. I knew that everyone was trying to be nice and shower me with everything, but I had a strong urge to get going and it was noticeable. Joe, at one point, said, "Why the hell do you want to go back?"

66 / A Knave Among Knights in their Spitfires

ESSEX FLIER
HOME ON LEAVE FROM OVERSEAS
JANUARY 1944

PO Jerry Billings R.C.A.F., of Essex, who has returned home for a month's leave after two years in England and Malta, is shown above looking over his log book, with his parents, Mr. and Mrs. J. D. Billings. PO Billings was shot down twice over Malta and rescued by naval patrol boats. Photo appeared in the Windsor Star about 1944.

What could I say? Here I was at 21 years of age, dedicated to the bloody war, and trying to explain my feelings. How little did he or anyone here know how strong my ties with the war had now become. I had lost many real close friends, exceptional pilots all, willing to give their lives without hesitation to protect your tail or give cover while you engaged the enemy. It was nice, I suppose, to go downtown, have a few beers, a fat meal, burp a bit, and then retire with all lights ablaze to a clean soft bed. How absolutely boring. How little did they know or how little did they really care for the guys still fighting.

Of course, my father never appreciated this type of life, especially uniforms, but we will come to that later.

I finally left this sheltered atmosphere with my sister Erla, who was travelling via train to Halifax to join her husband, and I arrived finally by boat (Halifax to Glasgow) back in the U.K. after nine days on the bloody ocean. How comforting it felt when I saw the coast of England. At last, I was home again.

I joined 401 Squadron the very next day, much to the annoyance of a transit officer, for I simply got off the train and disappeared. Lorne Cameron had now become C.O. of 401 at Biggin Hill, and he said, "Relax. Let's go and see W/C Buck McNair, 'The Boss.'"

When I entered McNair's office, with a log book in hand, he said, "Hellow, Jerry. Don't worry about H.Q. I'll fix that up. And good flying".

In later years I was to ask McNair, by then a G/Capt. in London, England, if he could help in transporting a Spitfire (dual) from the U.K. to Canada. He said, "Jerry, all of the old boys, I'm afraid, are gone, and we have nothing left but career climbers."

Upon arriving at Biggin Hill in 1944, I was given a Spit Mk Vb, with clipped wings and a cropped blower (carburetor) for a bit of practice. We referred to these Spits as clipped, cropped and clapped. A few days later I had my first trip in a Spit Mk IX, truly the best mark of Spitfire for combat. The Mark V was a real beauty if one wished to do an aerodrome beat up of low-level precision aerobatics.

I took off for a squadron assessment, led by a F/Cmdr Bob Hayward. These trips were aimed at sorting out the better pilots from the chaff.

Hayward called me into line astern and said, "O.K., see if you can follow me."

I simply moved into close line astern and followed through. After a few loops and rolls, he throttled back and weaved a bit, looking around and said, "If you know where I am, join up."

I pulled out and up in tight formation and said, "O.K., let's do something." Whereupon he replied, "It's O.K. The drome is at 3 o'clock. Press on and I'll see you later."

Rather disappointing to me at the time. I rolled away and turfed over to Redhill, where I tangled with two Spits for 15 minutes over aerodrome. It felt real good to have air under my arse again, and this mark of Spit handled well with bags of power.

401 Squadron at this point was involved in sweeps to France — the Lille and Dreux areas — but we saw no great intercepts or rendezvous with the Hun as in Malta.

One day over France, George Beurling, who was on 412 Squadron, simply pulled out of formation, pulled his nose high, give a quick squirt, and down came a Hun — to all of 412 pilots' surprise.

I used to talk to George often at the local fish and chips shop; his main desire was to get Spits with 90-gallon extra tanks and head inland, as we had done in Sicily, to pick off training schools in France. Or, if he could only organize a section of Mustangs, with their fuel and long range we could have a ball.

"You know, Jerry," he said. "I know we'll have an invasion to fly in, but wouldn't it be good to tool off inland and raise hell."

His wishes never came true, as he was posted, tour expired, to return as a veteran at twenty-one years of age to Canada.

People just never understood him, nor do they to this very day. Saddled with the name of "Screwball", this man was far above the average, an exceptional pilot who was a delight to fly with, a man who was extremely careful and very cautious. In order to shoot accurately, complete mastery of the machine is a *must*, no slip or skid allowed or one's bullets would not strike their mark. A pilot not in total control of his aircraft was no more accurate than a gun barrel wavering in a shaking hand. My impression of the snides slung at George was that they were merely the product of professional jealousy, nothing more.

George left the wing, and I had no other contact with him until the spring of 1948, when he spoke to me from Montreal of the Israeli war and the procedure to follow to join. A few days later I heard of his death in Campino, Italy. This, of courses, squashed all chances of joining that group. But more of that later.

When I joined 401 Squadron there was a glaring resentment towards anyone from the Malta operation — mainly because those pilots had one hell of a lot more air battles under their belts. They were highly experienced in dogfighting because of that battle, as opposed to most accustomed to fighting alone, and were likely to peel off to engage the enemy rather than set him up for the vying commander or squadron commander to shoot down. I suppose those who stayed behind also were concerned that those from Malta, with their experience, might advance in rank more quickly. Even today at reunions, the Malta guys, those who are left, stay a bit aloof.

In Malta, standard pair procedure was the order of the day, given the lack of pilots. In England, the 12-plane formation of the squadron — three sections of four line-astern — still existed. This was, to my mind, an extremely safe formation for the squadron leaders and the flight commanders. The number 4 of each section, especially of the outside section, were sitting ducks. The term was "Tailend Charlie". This position was invariably given to a new, inexperienced pilot, who had the impossible task of keeping the squadron in view *ahead* of him while keeping the air clear from attack from *behind* him. Many, many Tailend Charlies were shot down, while the squadron commanders kept their skins. A terrific sacrifice. The four plane line abreast was safe for ALL. However, by now, in England when a four plane formation took off, it was in finger four, which still leaves the number 4 open for attack, not covered completely as he is too far back. Whenever I was in this type of formation I simply came up into line abreast anyway.

69 / Chapter 6

401 Squadron, Tangemere, U. K. Prior to "D" Day.

"D" Day plus ONE. I had just returned to the U. K. in Spitfire Y - O - D having just shot down a Junkers - 88 over the beachhead.
This was the same Spitfire I was shot down in on July 1st. 1944

Unlike in Malta, a great rivalry was always present between squadrons in the U.K., and you referred to the others as a bunch of turkeys. A bomber type was always looked down on, as most had trouble with a single-engined fighter, but a fighter pilot had absolutely no problem with a bomber. The fighter pilot, of course, wore his tunic with the top button undone, which established his identify as a fighter pilot.

The quarters and Mess hall at Biggin were very good, by far the best I had lived in to date. From Biggin Hill flew most of the greatest pilots ever to strap a Spit or Hurricane to his back. Biggin was on a small hill, and as soon as you became airborne, you would be out over a steep cliff.

Grissle Klersey, I suppose, could be tagged as the character of the squadron, what with his long, blond, curly hair and the wedge hat donned somewhat in the middle of the curls, his high black boots with his pants tucked inside and his long white socks rolled out over the top. His tunic was always lightly disheveled, with the left side pocket torn and hanging; I never saw it repaired. Gris used to play the piano endlessly, chording and punching out a tune, sometimes with two fingers as Chico Marx used to do. Gris was a complete master at the keys.

When Grissle's turn as duty officer came up this was something to behold. Gris stood out on the parade area while the squadron ground personnel milled around waiting for Grissle's "supreme command" to fall in for inspection. Fantastic, I thought. Art Bishop said to me, "Look at this. Christ, just watch this. Have you ever?"

Old Gris stood at attention, a solid officer, looked toward the men and called for "Marker".

The squadron sprang to attention and marched smartly to Gris for him to position himself for others to follow. The supreme commander cried, "Squadron, fall in." At this, the airmen snapped smartly into position.

Grissle stood there in his battle garb, shaking his head, saying, "Won't do, chaps. Do it again."

Bishop and I exploded. Old Gris turned to us and said, "You bastards, scram. How can I conduct an inspection with clowns around."

It was priceless.

We used to receive boxes of chocolate from somewhere, and, with Gris around, you could enter the flight room to gaze upon a box of chocolates, each pressed in by a thumb to squash it unappetizingly. Grissle only liked hard centers, and it was his method of finding them.

Our squadron doctor had a Spaniel dog which he had trained to do tricks, including "addition", and "subtraction", and "square root", with the use of blackboard. The doc would place the number, and the dog, Dinghy, would bark out the answer — in response to some signal, I assume. Then one evening when we were in Maidstone, after we had retired quite late, Grissle heard a rooster crow outside the hotel and he went out and caught it. He decided for some reason that it needed a bath. He promptly took it to the sink and began the chore. Not to be outdone by the doc and his dog, Gris asked the rooster, "What's two and two?" He squeezed the rooster four times and it let out four squawks. "Bloody good, old cock," he said, "Now you can go." He put the rooster down, and one can imagine the mess as this disheveled, water and soap-bogged rooster rushed away down the hall.

Harry Dowding visited us one day from his aerodrome and told of an experience he had while on gunnery. The squadron commander had a large Land Rover, and when this vehicle departed for the local pub, the entire pilot group would swarm onto the set of wheels, hanging from the headlights, tailgate, and every spot that gave a handhold. Arrival at the pub was accomplished without incident other than the overheating of the radiator. When "time" was called in the pub, all piled on the Land Rover to go. The C/O, remembering the steaming radiator, ordered each pilot onto the front bumper to relieve himself, thereby gaining the required cooling liquid. I guess the smell was terrific, but it gave sufficient cooling effect to allow their return to base.

On the 28th of April, we were dive-bombing the rail yards at the Carentan Marshes area in Normandy, when F/O Bill Cumings went straight in for no apparent reason. Flak, we thought. We carried out a second trip of dive bombing that day with nothing of interest to record.

For the next two days a 45-gallon tank was slung under the belly of our Spits and we escorted Marauder bombers to Dreux.

The 30th of April gave me quite a scare. We had been briefed that, when dive-bombing, don't throttle back but go in fast and out fast to avoid the wall of flak. To date we were losing pilots — we thought because of flak. Before rolling over at Dieppe to bomb, I put on full power and was really driving along. Lorne Cameron and the rest had already gone down to drop their bombs. Doing well over 360 mph., I half-rolled and went down vertically. My speed hit over 500 mph and just would not go any faster. The pressure on the controls was extremely heavy. I had lost my target under my nose, so I spiralled to starboard 90 degrees and picked it up again, dropped my bombs, at the same time opening up my guns. The bloody Spit at this point gave a violent jerk forward and began to buck like a horse. Rolling the elevator trim back slowly had no good effect; movement of the elevators seemed to agitate the response. Thinking that I had rolled the elevator trim too quickly, I rolled it forward again and repeated the pull-out procedure. No good response. I was simply thrown about the cockpit, smashing my left shoulder against the door so hard that it moved the canopy off its rail. Then I tried exercising throttle and pitch, then both in sequence with the control column. Time for me was running out fast. I even tested my gas to check the content. What more to do? My pull-out height now was becoming critical. In desperation I wound the rudder trim full left. At this point the Spit flicked to the right in a screaming steep turn, leaving me about 150 feet from the deck, to appear as though I was looking at the bomb damage. (Deurling had a similar incident when he half-rolled over France after a 190.) My left arm was quite sore, and I was breathing very heavily.

Someone in the section said, "Where's Jerry?"

He was answered by another saying, "I don't know. Can't see him. I think he went straight in."

I was too shaken and out of breath to correct anything over the R/T. I checked the aircraft for damage, found it O.K., and proceeded to climb out over Dieppe. This, of course, was a great error. The Hun threw everything my way. Flak was bursting below, above, and all around me. I was split-arsing all over the sky.

I finally gave Cameron a call, saying, "I'm O.K. and am climbing out."

He said, "Don't climb out until you're past the coast. "

Too late, Lorne, I thought. I'm right in the middle.

I received no hits from any of this.

I ran through the stall procedure over Tangemere aerodrome. On landing, we discussed my problem and concluded that the rudder had something to do with the pull-out control.

We flew more escorts with the Marauder bombers to Lille. On the 2nd of May, F/Lt Koch crashed, hurting his back and taking him off Ops.

Someone came up with the idea of carrying 1,000-pound bombs. Lorne took off with one and dropped it off the isle of Wight. I was the second to do so, and found that the old Spit was sluggish and wallowed about. Red Asheley was next. As Red dove to drop the bomb, he pulled out prior to release. The bomb, however, carried on its trajectory, tearing off the belly of Red's Spit with it. This apparently stopped the nonsense of 1,000 pound bombs, for we never saw them again.

On the 8th of May we were flying in the Rouen area, when Bob Hamilton and I saw Tommy Dow Biggin's Spit hit and prang in that area. He became a prisoner.

On the 10th of May, Bob and I were flying as a section on a sweep to the Le Treport and Lille area. We were at low level, and we came across an aerodrome. Old Hammy went screaming across the drome, shooting the hell out of the strip, while I stayed high, hoping to draw the flak. I saw the telltale white glycol smoke come from his Spitfire, and he called, saying that he was hit. Bob pulled up and baled to become an evader.

On the 15th of May we were again over the Lille/Le Treport area, when old Sid Mills was hit, and he too baled out to become a prisoner.

On the 19th of May, we were sweeping France and ran into considerable flak. I was flying beside W/C Keefer, when the CO of 411 Squadron, Norm Fowlow, received a direct hit — one moment a Spitfire in full flight; the next, nothing but a cloud of smoke.

Throughout the month of May we flew many sweeps to the Lille, Dieppe, Dreux, and Le Treport areas without hardly seeing the Huns.

On the 30th of May, F/O Cohen had engine trouble while returning from France. He elected to bale out from 33 feet, but failed in his attempt. He went in just short of the English coast.

I received a couple of days off here. Dick Cull and I took the Auster squadron playabout aircraft to Biggin, intending to spend a few days in London. This was June 5th. That night at 10:00 old Cameron was on the horn to me at the Regent Palace, saying: "Bag your ass back here or you are going to miss it."

Before first light on the 6th of June, Cull and I were on our way to Tangemere for the D-Day Invasion.

The bloody weather was terrible on our way to Tangemere. We encountered very low clouds and had to hedgehop in order to get to the aerodrome. White invasion stripes had appeared on all the planes overnight.

We arrived late, however I was able to get in one trip over the beach head. The scene was terrific. I have often said in later years that even a millionaire could not have bought ringside ticket such as I had. From the U.K., stretching all across the Channel to Cherbourg, France, was a steady stream of boats, tugs drawing floating docks, and aircraft covering the whole shamozzle. One did not have to worry about direction or one's position; the wake of the invasion pointed clearly from the U.K. to France.

Balloon cables were a hazard, flown from the many boats. The weather, as usual, was wretched, with the low clouds, winds and drizzle — a typical European day, I thought.

We flew beneath the clouds and patrolled the beach. Our sector was Gold Beach. For identification purposes, the beach area had been divided into various sectors, the easterly beach being code-named Sword, where came to land the 6th British Airborne Division, 4th Armoured Brigade, 51st Highland Division, 27th Armoured Brigade, 3rd Infantry Division and 1st Special Service Brigade Commando. Next to the westward was Juno Beach, landing zone for the 4th Special Service Brigade Cammando, Canadian 2nd Armoured Brigade, and Canadian 3rd Infantry Division. Next was Gold Beach and the 49th Infantry Division, 7th Armoured Brigade, 8th Armoured Brigade, and 50th Northumbrian Division. This was the beach with which I would become most familiar, being adjacent to B4 air strip at Beny-sur Mer, which, became our base of operations a few days later. Next were the landing zones of the U.S. Army. At Omaha Beach landed the 2nd Infantry Division, 29th Infantry Division, 1st Infantry Division, and 2nd Armoured Division. Utah was the westernmost beach where crossed the 9th, 79th, 4th, and 90th Infantry Divisions.

A hell of a lot of ground fighting was going on as I flew over Gold and Sword areas — homes and buildings inland burning or smoking, endless bomb bursts everywhere, men and equipment scattered all to hell, and bodies floating all along the coast. As I swept inland just above the rooftops I saw many civilians waving to us with towels or aprons in hand. Of course, at this point, I truly appreciated the female populace. And why not? They always seemed to have the warmest welcome.

We tooled around the area, going at will here and there, and in general surveying the whole scene. It was fantastic.

When one flew out to sea one had to keep a canny eye out for the bloody balloon cables. I had hoped to hell we would get into the Abbeville guys, but I saw no enemy aircraft and fired no shots of any kind.

The excitement of the day followed our landing, and of course we detested the oncoming darkness. The next A.M. I was awake before dawn and ready to get back in it.

The squadron took off en masse, and I joined up with F/O Doug Husband. We arrived over the beach and set up a patrol inland around Omaha Beach. The squadron was heading east, Doug and I trailing slightly. I was covering Husbands's tail when I saw an aircraft strike a balloon cable off the cost and spiral to the ground.

I called enemy aircraft at 7 o'clock. Breaking to port I passed over Doug and headed for the aircraft and now identified them as JU 88's, about twenty of them.

I approached the enemy from their 10 o'clock position and broke to the left into the nearest 88. Half way through the turn I rolled to the inverted position and came around to port, closing in nicely. I held my fire till 800 yards and came boring in. At about 900 feet I saw one body leave the aircraft, and a chute began to deploy. I had insufficient time to give him a squirt, for almost immediately another body came past, again surprising me completely. I was about 400 feet from the JU 88 now and my sights were full, with the starboard engine in the centre. I opened up, holding a very steady and careful course, and with no more than 20 rounds of all my guns, fired. The starboard engine simply burnt into flames, the wing at the fuselage blew, and the whole Jesus wing folded. I pulled up hard and to the starboard to see old Husband blast his 88 to hell. Doug confirmed my 88 as he had seen me prior to his attack.

During my attack I was so intent on killing this bird that I was twice surprised by the baleouts, and neglected to cover my tail or keep a look out at the surrounding sky. Consequently, by the time I looked about, I could find neither the other Huns nor Spits. The bloody clouds were low, and I decided to climb on top. Climbing hard, I broke out at 5,200 feet.

The sight I had when I popped out of the cloud terrified me. The sky was loaded with Hun fighters. I searched desperately for at least one Spitfire, but saw none. I had broken cloud right under a section of FW 190's. I turned in behind the Number 4 on the port side of a section and gave him a quick squirt from long range.

Because I was alone, I quickly broke starboard and came around 180 degrees into a position on another 190. From astern one quarter I gave a burst then pulled up vertically, did a half snap to starboard and pulled through.

Mrs. Billing's boy at this point decided to get the hell out. I entered cloud almost immediately and popped out beneath the cloud going like the clappers and in a 60-degree turn attitude. At once I saw an aircraft off my port wing and I broke into him.

Recognizing it as a Spitfire, I straightened out and waggled my wings. The Spitfire joined up and I signalled a return to Britain. H gave me the old thumbs up and we flew in battle formation, line breast, all the way home.

This pilot turned out to be Phil Charron of 412 Squadron. I had noticed that his gun patches were blown off, verifying that he had fired his guns at something.

Phil claimed a JU 88 on this trip.

For my part, as I learned months later, I had been mentioned in Dispatches.

Upon my landing I found the squadron already home. They had been harassed by some USAF Thunderbolts (they were a continual problem) during their encounter. Lorne Cameron had shot down two JU 88's. Art Bishop, son of Billy Bishop of World War I fame, and Scotty Murray had shared one. Dick Cull got one, and old Halcrow claimed a probably. Not too bad, I thought, for being plagued with very rotten weather. I had no other trips that day. It was our squadron's first encounter for the D-Day-plus-one invasion.

It was dark when we left the beaches, and half way home my bloody electrics went out. I tagged onto the tail of the nearest Spit and followed him in very close, line astern. At this point I was completely lost, no radar and no idea where I was.

75 / Chapter 6

B4 Airstrip, Normandy, June 1944. Bishop - Jerry - Klersey - McRae

Remains of Spitfire Y - O - D that I was shot down by " Flak " 1st. July, 1944
(Note strength of tail plane).

The Spit pilot did not know I was there, and I was not about to tell him. We flew on and on, and at one point I saw a red glowing indent light go by, but it was above my cockpit. Christ, I thought, are we upside down? Shortly afterwards, my guide throttled back and at once his wheels popped down. I slid out to his starboard and dropped full flap and wheels. I then saw the six ground lights indicating his landing path. I saw him pass the first light then I put my Spit in a great sideslip and landed blindly straight ahead.

I came to a stop, turned right, and saw nothing familiar. Even my compass told me nothing. North did not mean a thing. I was lost completely.

I taxied slowly ahead, and finally decided, rather than hit something, to stop and shut down.

When I got out of the cockpit all was dark, no lights, no noise, no mother, no nothing, so I jumped up on the engine and began yelling.

In a few minutes I could hear the engine of an approaching vehicle. It pulled up and I said: "Where the hell am I?"

"Tangemere," was the answer.

"For Christ's sake, "I said. "OK, I'll start up. Lead me back to 401."

I must say here that the feeling of being completely lost is most terrifying, and a feeling I have had on only one other occasion.

We patrolled the beaches on the 8th of June, and lost P/O Shorty Marshall somewhere over Omaha.

On the 11th of June, we were patrolling the Gold area and flew low over our new drome, B4, in France. The engineers were coming along fine, and we would soon be able to operate from France, doing away with this over-the-water trip.

411 Squadron lost a pilot to flak.

I did one sweep on the 12th of June. Although bogeys were all around, I sighted none. The battle on the ground looked fierce, explosions and fires everywhere. Sure would not want to be down there, I thought.

I experienced r.p.m. problems the next two days and stayed with the machine to get it sorted out.

On the 15th I was off again with Hap Kennedy, Bishop, and Klersey, patrolling the Le Havre and Caen area. We landed early and heard that 421 Squadron, operating from a makeshift strip in France, had run into 20-plus, destroying ten ME 109's in the encounter. Old John McElroy got one, but he was slightly hurt in the action.

On the 18th of June we landed on our new strip. On a quick patrol, Klersey and I ran into some 190's but were unable to engage them.

On the 19th of June, Hap Kennedy and I looked up from our drome to see an ME 109 screaming across the sky, hotly pursued by a Spit. Old Hap was screaming, "Get the bastard! Get him!" and was almost to his knees assisting. The bloody ground Ack Ack opened up and, to our complete amazement, shot the Spit down. Obviously their deflection was late, catching old Harry "Babe" Fenwick head on.

Babe came from Leamington. I had often played basketball against him. Babe had had a trying life, being adopted as a youth, I was told.

Beny-sur Mer's graveyard at that time was only blessed with six bodies. Babe was the seventh to be lowered by a makeshift strap jigged up by my rigger.

We saw very little action for the next few days other than bombing and strafing targets at random. A hell of a lot of flak though.

Because of B4's closeness to the front line, we could only take off toward the sea and land from that direction. I would sit under a tree and watch Typhoon diving and firing their salvo of rockets in the distance. What a ringside seat, I thought. Kind of scary though, as a section of four would go in and only three would reappear.

On the 21st, old Klersey and I were sent out with bombs to drop on a bridge southeast of Cobourg. After we dropped our lot, Grissle and I tooled off to the east of Caen and, while we were driving along, we spotted a couple of dispatch riders on motorbikes.

I peeled off and came in behind one. I opened up my machine guns, under-leading him, and when I saw my machine gun bullets strikes appear behind him, I pressed both cannons and machine guns, allowing pressure off the control column, raising the nose slightly. The rider was hit at my harmonization range, and he blew apart, pieces going everywhere.

We pulled up to starboard, and Grissle called that he had spotted some 109's. We roared further east and tangled with four light-coloured ME 109's. Grissle was busy to my left, and I broke around, avoiding an attack by an aggressive Hun. I was able to get a long astern one-quarter burst at his pal but saw no indication of strikes. The enemy broke off, and Grissle and I returned to B4.

Inspecting my aircraft, I found holes indicating that I had picked up some flak somewhere.

On the 25th, my second sortie that day, I was flying as No. 2 when we were bounced in the fading light by some FW 190's. Scottie Murray got a good shot at one, while I rolled to starboard and got a quick squirt from a 45-degree angle at a passing 190. No other action occurred except ground Ops were quite confused, and to this date I am sure they did not believe what we saw. On landing I simply ignored all briefing (as always), which generally led to too much emphasis being placed on one's activity. As old George once said, "The bloody medics and boffins will ground you for the slightest thing. Best to turn away and say nothing to anybody." I agree.

On the 27th, we were scrambled to intercept 30 plus. Lorne Cameron was leading and we spotted a gaggle heading east. We pursued them for some 15 miles and I could not quite understand why Lorne was holding back. I called him and said, "Let's get into them"

He replied, "I'm balls out."

"Well, I am not," I said and rammed my throttle full. The old Spit leaped ahead and I accelerated well past the squadron. (Lorne said later that great gobs of smoke belched from my aircraft.) I was closing in nicely behind two 109's when BANG came a hell of an explosion in my engine. I throttled back quickly and nursed the old Spit back to B4.

On landing I found that my boost aneroid had stuck open on my supercharger, allowing me about half as much boost over the maximum that was tolerable. I had really been travelling for a few minutes.

W.C. Keefer got a 109 on that day.

My second trip on the 27th was a patrol over Juno. We sighted some ME 109's, but they entered cloud. Although the range was excessive I gave a quick squirt at one just before he entered. Obviously well out of range, for nothing came back out of the cloud.

On the 28th I went to the U.K, in an Anson with old Art Bishop to pick up some much needed Spitfires.

We returned to B4 early on the 29th. That afternoon I flew an armed re-con to the south of Caen without incident.

The 30th saw Grissle and me off on a bombing sortie south of Caen. We were at 8000 feet when we rolled over to go down. A I could see was a wall of black and red flak. I called Grissle and said, "That is too thick for me. I am pulling off."

We pulled to port and flew inland to drop our eggs on a small convoy. Grissle received quite a few flak holes even at that height.

Soon after we arrived in France at B4, Beny-sur Mer, Old Rastus Sinclair and I found that the army personnel never used keys to secure their jeeps. To ensure that no one stole their equipment, they removed the distributor rotor. Of course, our next move was to steal the C/O's rotor. We took a trip to Bayeau and approached a likely jeep having some army markings. The rotor worked, and we drove madly to B4, hid the jeep in the long grass behind our tents, and painted it with our C/O's markings. For gas we took the 120-octane fuel used in the Spits. It was quite powerful and used to burn out the valves quickly. We simply stole another army jeep and repainted it.

Many of the pilots captured German motorcycles. Jack Hughes had gotten a large powerful machine. I had a two-stroke job that I could run beside and, when it got going, simply hop on with no problem. Because of the power of Jack's, and his being scared of it, Jack and I traded. On one occasion I was going so fast on Jack's bike that my eyes were full of tears and I could hardly see. I drove the bike back to the strip and the last I saw of it, it was learning against a tree. I decided the jeep was safer.

One must remember that the percentage of pilots "being Sgt." far outnumber officers in Malta.

It was not uncommon to complete sections of 4 aircraft made up of Sgt. with a Sgt. leading. The last two and a half months on Malta I was leading as Sgt. with Sgt. and officers making up the team. If anyone saw an enemy aircraft, regardless of his position in the flight, he could peel off and attack, not so in the UK. If you were a #2 or 4 in line astern formation and saw an aircraft, you reported it and the lead would say, "I see it, I'm going in, cover me."? George Beurling when on a Canadian Squadron with Dean Dover (the F/Cmd) was put as #4 (a typical normal move when a new pilot joined the squadron). This would not have upset George as he was not saddled with the problem of leading a section as (line astern) demanded in the U.K., but to peel off and attack when his outstanding vision sighted the Hun. This situation was not realized by one of the C.O.'s that Beurling flew with on a squadron, when he returned to the U.K. Beurling was upset when he promoted him to a F/Comdr. position, there by taking away the freedom. I'm sure to this day, realization of that problem is not understood. It's a fact when a melee started you were "on your own anyway" at least any in dogfight I was ever in. They really did not appreciate peeling off etc., but it was war, and there was a Hun. Dogfights on my return to the U.K. and France (for me), were extremely rare.

It truly would have been exciting to have a section of 4 aircraft to wander at will, in, or around Abbeville area. Dave Fairbanks DFC/Bar on Typhoons was allowed this excitement and did extremely well. (But I shouldn't like Typhoons).

7. SHOT DOWN, ESCAPE AND EVASION

The first of July was low overcast and promised to be a dull day for flying. Tex Davenport had just returned from England with some bread (which was hard to come by) in his wings, so we were looking forward to dinner. Hap Kennedy, Jackie Hughes, Mournful McRae and myself as a section had just been relieved from 30 minutes standby and proceeded to pile into the lorrie, and the driver jerked us forward toward the mess tent. We stopped first at our tents, had a thorough wash (just over the fingertips and eyelids), then Hap and I strolled over to the mess. Here we found the C/O Cameron Grissle Kersey, Jerry Bell, Havers, and Art Bishop all crowded around Tex, listening to him shooting the guff. He was describing some sort of trash he'd had in England, when Hap said: "Come on, Jerry. Old shit-for-brains is off again." So we arranged ourselves in line for food.

I recall this dinner very clearly. The fellow had just purchased (i.e. taken) some beef from a local farmer, and we were having steak. Hap received his plate of meat, and I in turn took mine along with a couple of slices of good old bread. At last a square meal. I stopped and grabbed two handfuls of candy kisses and stuffed them into the inner pocket of my battle dress. I had always done this; it gave me something to munch on during the day. We had just sat down, and I was cutting my steak when the DIR came running into the tent and said: "Yellow Section, scramble."

Son of a bitch.

I really didn't know whether to stuff my steak into my pocket or not. While I debated, Hap said, "What do you think, Jerry?" So we tore out of the tent and bounded for the truck.

Arriving at our aircraft I found that mine was already started and ticking over. Lovely. I hopped in, buckled my parachute and straps, tore my hat off and donned my helmet, waving to my Erks. I taxied to the end of the strip, arriving at the same time as Hap and Mournful. Jackie was having some sort of hood trouble. I waved to Hap, "OK!"

Hap and Mournful hit the blue, followed by myself and Jackie going balls out. Jackie at this time signalled me that he was returning, so I joined the first two aircraft.

The cloud base was 1000 feet or lower, and our sortie was to patrol from B4 landing strip to twenty miles west in order to intercept some little job of 12-plus approaching the beaches. We patrolled the area twice, with Mournful nearest the beach area, then Hap, then me, my position being approximately 400 feet and over no man's land. Control called and said that the plot had turned back, but for us to continue patrolling. I thought: 'Damn me,' and we just left a good steak to patrol here.

My 180-degree turn off the west end on this patrol was bringing me over a heavily wooded area. This area seemed to me to hold a strange power within it. I could just see the Hun getting my range, height and speed perfectly. On the next 180 degree, I intended to make my turn towards the beach area but abandoned this idea as Hap started his turn.

I had just competed mine, and, while levelling out, wham! — like a pail of stones hurled at me. My motor blew up in my face, filling the cockpit with smoke and flames. I glanced out to my right and left, and noticed holes large enough to throw a dog through. My radiator temperature flicked off the clock, and the whole aircraft began to judder. I was blinded momentarily by the smoke, but remembered my height at approximately 400 feet. I flicked my radio button on and called Hap. "Hap, where's the nearest field? I've been hit and cannot see!"

Some clown pipes in and says, "Are you in Blue Section?"

"Bastard!" I called again and said, "Hap, is there a field close in front of me?"

He was just explaining the location of one when my radio went dead.

My heading was north, so I turned to the left and spied a field with cows in it, kind of marshy and with a small accompanying stream. I flipped my flaps down (my speed being high, I am sure they were inoperative), snapped my safety harness lock catch, and pulled my straps tight for a crash landing. Opening the hood by the jettison method, I spied several enemy troops just ahead and in the area of my intended arrival, so I opened up both machine guns and cannon at them. At intervals my engine seemed to be belching out great clouds of crap, allowing me to see my flight path only the odd second.

As the aircraft was juddering viciously I jammed the stick forward and noticed my speed, 160 mph. The earth now was rushing towards me, and my landing space was running short. I eased out and hit the deck at the same time, bounced, and pinned the aircraft down. Thrown forward, my head about to be bashed by our new reflector site, I turned my face to the left and received a hell of a bang on the right side of my head just above my eye. The port cannon dug in, and I was swinging into a Jesus circle to port. Bits of aircraft and my prop, along with great gobs of each, flew over a Christ half acre.

The aircraft settled amongst all the shit, smoke and fire. I opened my eyes and actually looked for the cloud to walk away on. None? So I scrambled out, tearing off my helmet and trying to grab my hat, when I heard 'Zing!' — rifle bullet scream over my head, and I realized my mistake.

During the crash I had opened my guns and literally sprayed the countryside, my guns still firing from my thumb pressure after the aircraft had settled. The enemy was now after revenge.

Forgetting about my hat, I dropped to the ground, my aircraft hiding me momentarily. I dropped my parachute, tore off my Mae West to carry with me — it was too big a yellow target to be worn — and placed my white scarf (which I had made from a parachute strip) in a sign of an arrow pointing northwest, then proceeded to go east in a half-crawl run manner.

My aircraft was smoking good now, and Hap had just completed a circle to starboard above. I waved to him and he turfed off.

I then hear the Hun holler, and they opened up a machine gun in my direction. I hit the dirt and crawled to a stream, where a small boat was tied off, about 50 feet from my smoking plane. This was fortunate. I began untying the chain with quick grabs, waiting for an explosion. I thought of the possibility of it being bombed so I would duck my head after each grab.

I then became aware of my wound, as blood was running from my head down my cheek and into my mouth. This blood was of an odd taste, as it bore with it a strong taste of gunpowder.

The chain fell free, and I clung on to my Mae West, for I cannot swim,, and scrambled aboard though the stream was approximately 18 feet wide, and I no doubt could have waded across.

To the east, about 50 feet down from where the boat had been tied, the stream branched off into another tributary. At the junction of the streams I jumped ashore and kicked the boat back across the stream.

I crawled along the most northerly bank and lay under the reeds (as Moses had done), submerging my body and pulling reeds over my face. The Hun had opened up on the surrounding district now, and I could hear more of them coming from the east and south.

The opposite shore was thick with high, heavy reeds, good for concealment. My site was low and flat as though it has been bashed down by a recent storm. My choices of spots proved to be quite wise. At this moment I could hear the Squareheads approaching. My head lay into the northeast. I glanced back over and saw, through the reeds, German infantrymen, five in number, walking in a single file approximately five feet apart. The third turned towards the river and myself, and aimed. "Burp Burp" — guns opened fire and sprayed the shore directly across from me.

I was so damned petrified that I could not have moved even if I had wanted to. They sure must have been blind, as I was shaking sufficiently for them to feel the earth tremble. I was actually trying to rise from the water and say, "Here I am. Don't shoot," but failed to raise so much as a finger. I also tried to talk to them, but no words would come out, although my mouth was open.

They turned away and continued this procedure for at least a half an hour, a most amazing ordeal. Through all the shooting the only thing that struck me were the empties ejected from the deadhead's guns.

I spent two days and three nights in the same spot. By this time the Americans had advanced a few yards, thus leaving me in the center of no man's land. All day I would hear the German heavy artillery open up, then 'Zing, zing, zing boom' land in Yankee territory; this being answered by 'Boom, zing, zing, zing' by the Yankee heavy stuff into German territory.

At two o'clock A.M. on the third night I deemed it safe to try to break through the *German-held* line. I wanted no part of an Yankee bullet if I were to stop one. After forming a mental position of German rifle fire and gathering stones to fling as far east and west as possible (to produce sentry fire), I decided on a course of about 135 degrees true from my present locale, and crawled on my stomach for endless hours until the fire was behind me. (The candy kisses proved to be good.)

I then proceeded east along a ledge. I came to a large oak tree, buried my gun at the base, and continued until I came to a large U-shaped building. I approached the southern end and started inspecting each room, for what I do not know.

Running parallel to this building was a drive hedged by a stone wall — as I was making my way to the northern portion I observed a faint cigarette glow ahead, and it was approaching. I lay down beside the stone wall, the night being pitch black, and waited.

Three German soldiers walked past me and entered this building. I could hear them ready themselves for sleep. I removed my shoes and crept as I have never crept to the southern part of the building. Then I ran like hell, stumbling, falling into a ditch of water, tearing my hands and continuing on till I was well clear of the building. I huddled in a dense growth for the remaining hours of darkness and tried to sleep. As usual it started to rain.

The next morning was lovely and the sun was very warm. I plowed on and came to a farm house, skirted it, and hid in the tall grass behind the farm. Here I rolled a spot flat, and took off my clothes to dry.

After a few hours I redressed and approached the farm house, carrying a large knife for security. As I scanned the house, a German officer driven in a sidecar of a motorbike stopped, entered the house, stayed approximately 10 minutes, he reboarded the sidecar and drove off. I then went to the front door, tried the handle, found it free, and charged in, only to be greeted by an empty room.

Going through the house I found two rooms in actual use. The larger one contained a desk stacked with papers of some sort. These I disposed of by hiding them in the yard outside.

I left the joint, taking with me a black, knitted sweater. Passing through the garden I picked a large cabbage head and gorged most of it. This burned my throat terribly.

As I walked through the fields I would come upon various types of wire, different in colour, some yellow, some blue, and others brown. I would cut these with my knife whenever I had the chance. It may have been my imagination at the time, but I am sure several large artillery guns ceased firing.

I finally arrived at a through highway and decided it was time to take to the main roads for a change.

Walking in a southerly direction I noticed the road curved to the right. Bordering this bend and possibility 600 feet ahead were the Germans. I had taken off my rank and pilot badges in the tall grass and buried them with my papers, and hid my officer's I.D. card folded in the belt sewn area of my pants. The only item I kept was my knife, comb and nail clippers. All other items had been discarded, except two escape pictures taken for that purpose.

The Germans were busy erecting a road block. I knew immediately that a retreat would arouse suspicion, so I racked my brain for an idea and decided that if they should ask for identify I would produce of my RAF pass in a quick movement and possibility baffle them?

As I approached I lengthened my stride, slobbered at the mouth, hunked my nose, and walked through the barrier. The Germans halted work for a moment, looked at me and turned in disgust (I almost made myself sick). What an invigorating moment. I dared not look back, as I had effectively, in fact, broken through the remaining segment of the enemy front line.

I carried on my southward trek for some time. As nightfall was approaching I decided to conceal myself somewhere for the night. The European peasants bundle together small twigs which they often use for brooms or fireplace kindling. I spied a large pile of these and began arranging an area, piling them around me, and settled in. As nightfall came so did the Hun, and I'll be damned if they didn't bed down in exactly the same area as myself. They pushed back the brush and uncovered holes in the ground that they had previously prepared as night shelters.

This must be one of the classic nights in the war, for I remained smack in the middle of German night camp, a prisoner they didn't know they had. I listened to their German natter until sleep took over.

The next morning I lay silently amongst the twigs, nor daring even to sneeze. At 1045 hours all was quite and I determined to leave this hideout. I was in the small village of Marigny, which had been evacuated. Eventually I found a school house. Going through a desk I found an old geography book and tore out the map of the local area. I was able to orient myself and to dream up some sort of orderly plan. My aim was to go to Tessy-sur Vire, some 50 km to the south. I had actually crashed just north of Tribehou.

On leaving Marigny I was approached by two German soldiers and taken into custody. As a local farmer tantalized them with bread, beef and some good wines, they locked me in a type of chicken pen so they could eat. With my knife I took out the nails which held the hinges and promptly left the area, heading in a southeast direction.

I walked toward Tessy-sur-Vire but found that my feet were now beginning to blister. My shoe leather had turned hard in the hot sun, giving me added trouble.

Just as I was entering Tessy, another Hun stopped, asked me a question, and, because I did not answer, he pointed his gun at me and motioned for me to back into a corner of a building. We were quite close to each other, and he handled his defense sloppily, I thought. He kept looking over his right shoulder, calling to someone. I eased my hand into my shirt and grasped the handle of my knife. He appeared to receive no response from his comrade and was looking very nervous. He turned his head again, at which time I drew my knife and leapt to thrust it to its hilt into his midsection. Immediately I rolled to my back, completing a somersault, twisting the knife out of his belly. He jerked forward and fell gasping and hollering for help. Knife in hand, I took off as a deer, leapt over a hedge and ran low to backtrack in the direction from which I had come.

I thrust the knife into the ground to wipe it clean, and stowed it back under my shirt. I rounded a building and bounded east toward the road. As I ran I took off my tunic-covered sweater, turned it inside-out, and rolled my pantlegs up to the knees. I entered the road and proceed in a casual long-stepped walked toward the area from which I had just escaped. One Hun was facing in my direction, while the original group was dashing to and fro, jabbering away to each other. I had not realized at the time how many Huns were about. I pointed back to my right, and the Hun nodded his head in thanks..

I entered Tessy-sur-Vire from the northwest and came into the square of the village. Several people milled about in the vicinity of the meat shop. I waited until the shop was empty, then approached the "fat" proprietor. When I said, "Canada pilot," he paced and began to shake. Another Frenchmen entered, and it became bedlam. Too much activity here. I proceeded to leave, and the man who had just entered motioned to me to walk round the corner. This chap gave me an old brown fedora and some raw eggs. He kept saying, "Beaucoup de Boche," and he shooed me away.

I didn't learn until many years later that the headquarters for the Germans was right across the street.

I left Tessy, hungry and most reluctantly, to proceed westerly on the main road towards the coast. My plan now was to go to Mont St. Michel — miles away. I thought that I could steal a boat and perhaps row toward Britain. As I look at it today, I must have been absolutely mad.

My purpose in choosing Mont St. Michel was because of the sea tides. One can only reach the area when the tides go out; once there, you were committed to stay until the tides changed. I believe the Hun would not wish to stay there under those conditions, bearing in mind the progress of the front.

My trek along the highway was killing. My throat was parched, I was hungry, and my feet blistered to the point of bleeding. I came upon a small stream near Maupertus, where I stopped and took off my shoes and socks to bathe my feet. This was a great error. The cold, dirty water made them ache more, and the blisters were unbearable. Only with extreme difficulty was I able to replace my socks and shoes. Pulling on the shoes literally brought tears to my eyes, and it was with great effort that I compelled myself to continue walking. I could have given up, but there was no one to give up to. No one, I am sure, can even imagine this situation unless he has himself actually suffered in this manner, starved, lost, dead tired, with a parched throat, desperate for water, scared, lonesome and thoroughly depressed. To this day I often think back to realize how even a friendly wag of a dog's tail or a nod from a stranger can lift one's shoulders and give a shot of adrenaline to press on. I am so pleased that while in this crazed state of mind I was not put in the situation of having to use my knife again against anyone, for I was keyed for survival at any cost and would have used it.

Dog tired, I troddled on toward Hambye, and as I reached the outskirts I checked the sun (God, how comforting to have the sun and its warmth) to find that only an hour remained till sundown. I decided to hide off the road and spend the night there despite a great urge to press on into the village in search of food and water.

I walked south off the road and began cutting branches from a tree to lay on for the night. Nightfall came and I huddled down to get some rest. I slept in spurts in a sitting position beside an old tree. At about 2:00 A M I was awakened by the distant loud rumble of equipment. Frightened, I listened and waited. It began to rain. What next, I thought.

I then recognized the approach of a group of tanks. Christ. Surely they hadn't set a tank group after me. But sure as hell, just as the main group passed me, everything stopped. Much German conversation took place with a lot of running about.

What the hell should I do? Walk out with my hands up or stay put and be shot like a rat? I waited. To my relief the entire group started up and proceeded east to fade into the night. Why they should stop as they did, I'll never know, but it sure gave me a fright.

It rained like hell throughout the night, and I turned my face to the sky to catch every precious raindrop that I could. I woke next morning, drenched, cold, and very stiff, not to mention the stomach pain and parched throat.

Walking now like an old man by necessity, I entered Hambye. As I walked into the centre of the village, I noticed a lorrie of Hun soldiers with the leader standing in front, holding a map. This Kraut beckoned me to come over. I ignored him, hoping he would think I didn't hear him. But the next shout was a definite command and one I thought I should not ignore. I turned and walked toward him.

From his expression and map in hand, it was obvious that he was lost. Because his automatic was loose and situated on his die that was facing me, I had a side thought to grab the gun and shoot the hell out of the whole works, but abandoned this quickly. More troops than bullets in his gun.

I approached him slowly, then boldly turned his map in his hand, and with my left shoulder against his, pointed to our area then turned and pointed south, saying, *"Dix kilometres."*

He was so pleased at my assistance (obviously he was late) that he jumped aboard the lorrie and roared away in the direction I had indicated. Whew, I thought. What next?

I walked on, over my fright, but still confused, hungry and exhausted. When I reached the town of Bréhal I noticed an apartment door standing open. I entered the room and saw a woman standing beside a table. On the table was a plate with a piece of meat on it. I waked slowly in, while the woman's eyes began to look like wall clocks. I pulled my knife about and pressed forefinger to my lips. I really must have looked absolutely wild, with white glaring eyes and teeth, knife in hand, as a wild animal — or a person starving for food. My hair was matted, my face unshaven and dirty, and arse torn out of my pants. My tunic-covered sweater was damp and dirty, smelling I'm sure of the nights on the earth. I know had the woman screamed or objected I'd have thrust the knife, so desperate was I, but she stood rigid as I grabbed the meat and devoured it while facing her. Looking about I saw nothing else of use, so I backed slowly to the door and departed in the direction that I had come. I ran to the next corner and turned to head back in the opposite direction, when I head her scream blue murder.

I left Bréhal, heading for the coast and Averanche. As I entered the town of Granville it appeared to me to be deserted — not much activity except for a group of men working near some lorries and a building. I walked straight up to them and at that moment they stopped work to look up at a section of P38 Lightnings that were circling the area. In my best French I tried to tell them what they were, saying, *"P trois neuf."*

The one chap turned and sad, "Who are you? You speak English?"

I said, "Well, I'm Canadian and was shot down a few days ago near Caretan."

"How did you get here," he asked.

"I walked here. Why?"

"Oh no," he said. "We have been prisoners from Jersey Isles since 1942 and we work for the Germans. Those are guards over there."

"Christ". I said. I'd better get out of here."

"But how?" he said.

"The same way I came in. I going to walk straight out."

"They'll shoot you". he said.

"Maybe so, but I'm not staying here."

"Anything I can help you with?" he said.

"Yes, give my your socks, please. My feet are bleeding."

He sat down, took off his shoes and socks and then handed me his socks.

Thanking him, I turned and walked as I had entered Granville. I must say here, though, that I had my shoulder braced for a bullet the whole time that I walked away.

Leaving Granville I headed without reason back to Bréhal, entered the town and walked into a small cafe. A few people were in the cafe. Quiet settled over the room as I entered.

It was with great relief that I finally found someone willing to help me. I asked for a drink of water and pointed to the tap. Never in all of my life even to this day have I tasted water so beautiful. The first mouthful I swished in my mouth and spat out into the sink. The next I let trickle down slowly into my throat. With my head held to the ceiling, tears running from my eyes I began to feel again the sense of living and warm friendship. One can compare this to the feeling that one has when he is with the one he loves and gazes upon the face of his beloved to receive that mutual eye twinkling message. It just melts you inside, completely.

There was much commotion this time, throughout the building, the French folks really wound up. I noticed that security of the front door was activated. Excited, the townsmen asked me questions galore. I emptied my pockets by the table and produced out of the filth the strange contents to great gasps of astonishment. I indicated that I wanted something to eat, which they started to prepare. To my surprise they prepared to cook the food. God! Had they known how hungry I was they'd have given it to me raw.

The one older chap (his left hand had been amputated, replaced by a steel ring) indicated to me to have a wash and a shave. He must be joking, I thought, but they readied the warm water and shaving gear, so I shaved. Throughout this whole procedure and with every stroke of the razor, the whole room watched my every move, spellbound. My stomach actually rolled to the smell of all the cooking goodies. I have heard of torture before, but this shaving episode was something else.

Finally I was seated at a table, the food placed in front of me. I could not hold back and obviously ate as a mad starved animal. As I began to feel a satisfied sensation, I began to take in my surroundings. One of the first persons I saw was a young, shapely brunette. I must add here that even starvation did not dampen my instincts to admire the female sex. She stood there in utter amazement, tears in her eyes at the picture I was unfolding. This girl was name LeBlanchette and she was the one who later on was to bring goodies from the local bakery.

The entire group appeared to be headed by the armless man whose name was M. LeBourgois. They had summoned a young man, Jean LeBreton, who,

French/English dictionary in hand, began to communicate with me. I explained my situation to him, and he told me that I would be moved to another spot, just west of the town, and that M. LeBourgois would show me the way.

Things were looking better now, and I followed this man to a small cottage set back off the main road. The first thing that I saw was a bed. Man, I though, I can't believe it. I sat down as M. LeBourgois indicated that I should rest.

As I took off my shoes he glanced at my bloodstained socks, and winced as though in pain. When I began to peel the socks from my bloody, blistered fee, he said "Oh non," and indicated to me to stay put.

In a few minutes a woman, later to be identified as his wife, Mme. LeBourgois, entered with a pan of water, some clothes and ointment. This woman I shall NEVER forget. With the kindest, most tender touch of her hands she knelt at my feet and bathed each foot softly, stopping at intervals to wipe the tears from her eyes — the most touching thing as yet to happen to me. After the ointment was applied, I stood up again, walked towards her and kissed her on the cheek. She hugged me as though I were her own, then beckoned for me to get rest.

Mme. LeBourgois, I found, had two sons my age, one being away in the Merchant Marines, the other home in Bréhal. I lay in bed for days, recuperating, being fussed over like a king. Two breakfasts were given me, each by a shapely damsel, and I began to feel alive again. Jean LeBreton would visit daily to talk of the situation around us and to improve his English and my French. M. LeBourgois would come in, and by gestures we began to understand each other. His wife, Mme. LeBourgois religiously cared for my feet twice a day, and, upon completing the dressing, always took my shoulders, hugged and kissed me like a child.

During the second week of my stay, I was told of a man in the area who had just escaped from the Hun in Paris. He was from the Jersey Isles and been taken prisoner in 1942. This Jersey man was name Jean Marion.

By this time I was moved into another small cottage, home of a nattering redhead, having a room upstairs. I ate all my meals next door in M. LeBourgois' house. Jean Marion moved into the same cottage as me, mostly to satisfy the whims of the redhead, a convenient situation for him, I thought. Marion, however, was not satisfied with everything in general and continually urged me to depart this area. With a map he showed me Coutance Town. Just west of this town, he said, was a village of Coutainville. His plan was to position there with the French folks and sit it out, having in mind that the village was off the main coast and would be by-passed by the retreating Hun. He proposed that we go into the village of Bréhal, steal a bicycle each from the Hun soldiers (as they alone possessed means of transport), and that we should depart as soon as possible for Coutainville.

Perhaps it was my sense of security in this home, or perhaps the food, or the friendly presence of M. and Mme. LeBourgois, Jean and Marthe, LeBlanchette, but I was reluctant to go. The whole village knew of my presence, the local priest, the shoemaker, the barber who came to the house to trim my locks. Hell, I thought, I'm established here. I can wait it out. At any rate, I told Marion that I did not wish to join him, and that if he thought he should go to press on without me.

Earlier that week M. LeBourgois had arrived with an identification card which the locals secured from the body of a local type who was collaborating with the Hun and whom they had done away with. M. LeBourgois had the necessary green ink and I had the escape picture. I took great pains in completing the green circle of the stamp "Prefecture De La Manche" over my picture. I secured it on the identification papers. A neat job, I thought, viewing the results. Now I was legal and could offer something to the Hun if stopped. My alias was "Gerard Marion". By chance, I was to have the same last name as this erratic man from Jersey.

Jean Marion was so overconfident that he treated the Huns as low, illiterate dogs, and I thought he underrated their intelligence. This proved to be correct, as the next day, when he was stealing a Kraut's bicycle he was commanded to halt. He pressed on in his own fashion. There was a tattoo of the Hun's burp gun, and Jean Marion fell dead beside the road. So upset was the Hun, that he ran up to the body and screaming wildly in German, he kicked the body furiously. This put a damper on all activity. It took a few days for the town to carry on or forget.

By means of my new identification I was able to move about and actually draw rations from the Hun in the town. I worried, however, that my last name, being Marion, might cause questions.

A local radio repairman gave me a crystal, and with the necessary earphones and wiring, I rigged up a crystal set. For an aerial I wired onto the electric wiring (no electricity anyway) and could pick up the BBC clearly.

During the day, Old M. LeBourgois and I would walk to the beach and he would point out land mines planted by the Krauts. We would dig them up and replant them along the footpath to the billets used by the Huns. As evening came, we would drink wine, and there would be a loud Bang. M. LeBourgois would smile and say, "*Si bon,*" and we would clink glasses for another toast to a dead Kraut.

M. LeBourgois was a cagey old character, openly friendly to everyone. Most disturbing to me was that he would invite the Huns into the house and feed them and serve them local wines. I used to sit at the same table to clink glasses with these bastards as they drank and generally gloated and talked over the situation. When any of them spoke to me, M. LeBourgois would pipe in, saying "Monsieur Gerard, bicycle mechanic from St. Lo. He has lost his hearing because of the bombing of the city." St. Lo had been flattened by this point by both sides with all buildings demolished.

In the same home as M. LeBourgois there lived a man name Julian and his wife and son, Lucien. One day as we were walking along the road, a P47 of the Americans dove on a small bridge to bomb it. It aimed badly and the bombs fell in an open field. The Hun soldiers gather round, and as they approached, this boy of 9 or 10 year came to my side, grasped my belt, turning to me for protection against the

90 / *A Knave Among Knights in their Spitfires*

Art Bishop at Tangemere, U. K. 1944 prior to " D " Day, son of Billy Bishop W. W. I Canadian Fighter Ace.

Madame LeBourgois The lady that bathed my blistered and bleeding feet.

The LeBourgois family who took care of me with their neice.
The grave of Pascal LeBourgois. Mr. Pascal LeBourgois hid me and helped me with my escape, even with his left hand missing.

enemy. Little did he really know that I was as afraid as he, but his turning to me and not to his father gave me a rather possessive feeling and did, in fact, stimulate my ego, putting me again in a defensive mind, planning for survival if it should come to that.

Living in this manner for about a month gave me enough time to recuperate fully, and I actually put on weight. I had learned of the position of a large tank battalion to the south, which was gathering for a drive north. I was also daily plotting the Allied drive south. On the first of August we were told of the U.S. tanks just approaching Bréhal. As the first tank appeared, I greeted the commander with my I.D. and told him of the situation in the area and of the tank position to the south. I ran back to M. LeBourgois' cottage to give my farewell. He thrust a bottle of Calvados into my hand and I kissed them goodbye. It was quite difficult parting, as Mme. LeBourgois stood, shoulders down, wiping the tears from her eyes with her apron. What a woman.

Within a few hours I was spearheading in a tank toward the rendezvous of the hidden German tanks. Christ, I thought. What am I doing riding in a tank, guns going continually, penetrating father south than where I had come from? I told the commander. "Please stop. I'll show you on a map. For God's sake, put me on a jeep and head me back north"

I got my wish and was driven to the St. Lo area. In the village of Crenees we came under fire of snipers. We all dove for cover only to see a small girl of about 5 or 6 years run out into the open and point to the direction of the snipers — a fatal move for the child. The snipers opened up on her and she was blown, dead, backwards off her feet, a German slug through her chest. A great desire to rid France of these killers flared up in me. But what to do? I knew nothing of ground fighting. The U.S. troops dispatched a gun platform to the area. This unit was called "Chicago Organ," having several fast repeating type salvo guns mounted on the back of a truck. It pulled into position, and with a great salvo blew the snipers' tree to hell with a fantastic display of firepower.

Aboard the jeep again, I was driven to a makeshift H.Q. in the middle of the rubble of St. Lo. What a sight, dead bodies, cows, blown-up vehicles, household goods, everything littered the streets. I was questioned by a U.S. captain whom I told that I must get to my Squadron B4 strip at once.

He said, "I'm sorry, but you will have to wait until I get orders."

I wandered around outside until I spotted a sergeant in a jeep driving toward the tent. I hailed him, showed him my officer's I.D., and said I must be driven immediately to B4, Bény-sur Mer

"OK", he said. "Hop in".

I arrived at the squadron to be hailed by Kerlsey and Tex, and to hear that Scotty Murray, Hap Kennedy, Lorne Cameron and several others had also been shot down. Old McElroy was preparing to go to the U.K. for a short leave. I checked with the CO and was told that M.I. 9 had to check everyone evading. This found me on my way to the U.K. to be briefed by M.I. 9 (Military Intelligence).

Commandeering the jeep to the squadron and arriving without proper papers from the unit which had found me did not sit too well with M.I. 9. Why this? Why that?

And in general at first they thought me a spy planted in the organization. Then next day everything cleared up. I was allowed to press on to get reclothed and report to H.Q. London. Prior to going I looked up a Red Cross organization to get some pajamas and socks along with some underclothes. When they produced the goods, I found each item had a price on it. As I had yet to visit our pay officer at Knight Bridge, I was unable to pay. I said that I would return. My next stop was in a Salvation Army station. Here I found help. All of my needs were taken care of with a terrific meal thrown in as well. To this day I still repay this organization.

My visit to H.Q. was disappointing. I found that my flying operations were stopped short. Two tours of operation, plus my escaping and episodes behind the lines forbade me to fly in the Western Theatre again. How about chasing Buzz Bombs, I said. "No," was the reply, "You are posted home to Canada. You're finished."

I booked into the Regent Palace Hotel Square and ran into Barry Needham, who had also escaped after being shot down but had burns on his hands and face. The dead flesh gave a slight odor but we teamed up for a rest in good old London. On one occasion while drinking tea in the lounge of the Regent, two shapely blondes sat adjacent to us. They had a small carrying case which they sat down gently beside them. I spoke to the one, "If you girls have liquor in that bag, Barry and I know where to get the mix." They accepted without hesitation and opened the bag to reveal two bottles of Beefeater Gin.

Prior to leaving France, I thought I must have some souvenir from the unit on B4. I looked up my old Erk and asked him if I could borrow a hacksaw. With it hidden under my clothes, I inspected a Spitfire sitting at the back of the line and not completely operational. Once in the cockpit, I found the air pressure at only 20 pounds and proceeded to hack the Spitfire's control column from its securing base. I made very little noise, and no one seemed to be objecting. I shoved the control spade grip into my shirt and returned the saw. Today this grip stands mounted — Nelson Boose being the artist and carpenter — as a lamp end table in my house.

93 / Chapter 7

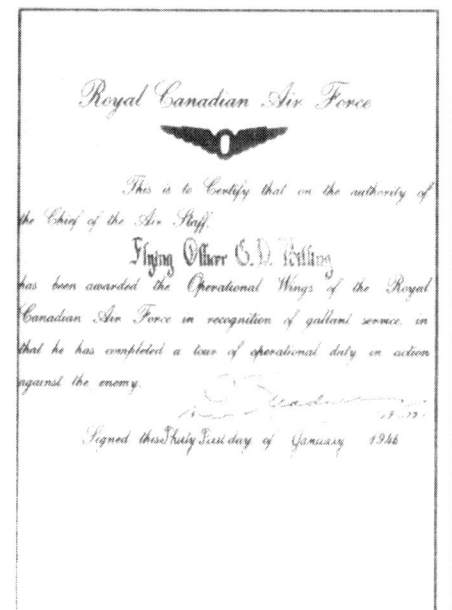

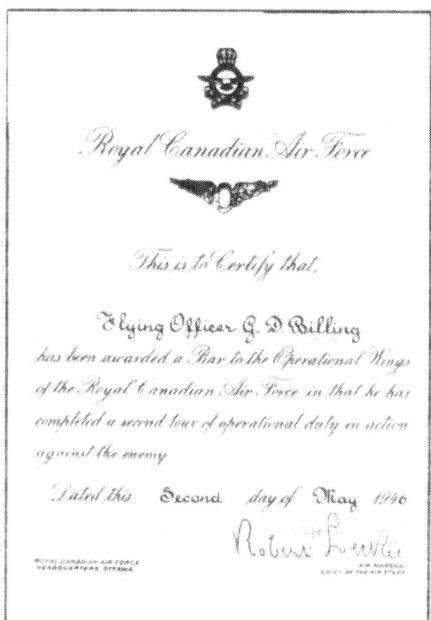

Certificates awarding Jerry Billings with his Operational Wings of the Royal Canadian Airforce and Bar having served two tours of duty in action.

Jerry by the grave of Jean Soyer who was kicked to death by the Germans

8. REPATRIATION AND DISCHARGE - CANADA

Because of all of the V2 bombing now occurring in London, I thought it best to approach H.Q. with repatriation plans and to get out of London. I was told to go to Glasgow, Scotland and there await sailing orders. Within the week I was again aboard a troop ship, tour expired, with memories of great pilots who would never grace the shores of Canada and Britain again.

My first arrival in Canada, in 1944, for a thirty-day rest leave, had been blessed with the red carpet treatment — photographers, news media, radio, VIP's from Ottawa. The town council had presented me with a wallet, a token of their gratitude.

My second arrival in Canada, I suppose, touched off a few memories. In the local Windsor newspaper I had been hailed as a hero for shooting down enemy aircraft, followed by the terrible news of Mrs. Billing's boy missing and believed killed, then the news that I was again safe in Britain. All of this never really entered my mind while it was happening, and I only became aware of it when I again returned to the Windsor area. But somehow this return was not as the first. There was no real clamoring to greet the war hero this time. Even after only one year, people were tired of the war and sick of heroes, who they thought felt the world owed them rehabilitation and an exceptional living. This time it was thirty days of rest and doing and going where I wished — no speeches or dinners or wallet from the local council or praise from the town merchants, who, prior to the war, made it a point to degrade a man further because of his social position and being unemployed and just plain broke.

I was granted a one-month leave then ordered to report to Uplands as an instructor on Harvard aircraft. I might say that this didn't sit too well in my craw. I entered the station at Uplands to find most of the pilots all pressed up in F/Lt. or S/L. rank milling around, grumpy as hell because more promotion was not coming as fast as they would like to have it. Coffee break was mandatory. How could I really fly here? I did not have the impression that I was better than any other pilot, but their attitude and general coolness toward anyone who had "Canada Badges" on his shoulder was very apparent. This was one thing that Air Defense buggered up badly and this business with the badges was responsible for highs and lows in morale throughout the bloody Air Force. If a pilot or aircrew stayed in Canada and did not leave the confines of the safe surroundings, he was not allowed to wear the Canada Badges on his shoulder, so the wearing of these drew attention to an aircrew who had served out of the country. You can guess the split among the pilots in the Officer's Mess. This became such a problem that in 1949 the order was changed and all personnel were ordered to don the badge. I recall in Trenton, Ontario in 1948 when pilots who were posted from Command to Station and back and forth again (without ever leaving Trenton) throughout the whole bloody war, took a Lancaster for a trip to England and back in order to qualify. I recall clearly when we presented these heroes with their badges at the bar in the Officer's Mess in Trenton. Old Don Lewis will recall this too, I know, for we dipped each set of badges in a mug of beer.

The only thing that perhaps gave as much attention to aircrew as the problem associated with the wearing of Canada Badges was that of being branded L.M.F. (lack of moral fiber). My first introduction to those three damning letters was when I joined the O.T.U. after returning from Malta. I knew of course that many, many chaps joined the Air Force/Navy ground environment just to beat their conscription call and enable them to select a station of their choice within Canada, but I really never was acquainted with a pilot who was not keen or did not want to go on Ops, so the idea of such a punishment never entered my mind until faced with its existence at Kirton-in-Lindsay. You could see those who had been labeled walking about, the outline of where the wings had been stripped off their uniforms still visible. The threat of those letters was like a hatchet over the head. The Army or Navy never had this punishment. Several aircrew types who were actually sick flew anyway to avoid being thought "not keen", and as a consequence got shot down, not responsive enough because of their illness. I flew a sweep over France when I could not move my left arm as the result of an inoculation we received in preparation for D-Day. The thought of being branded L.M.F. was a great threat, even though you were keen to fly. And to see a chap who was court-martialed, with his tunic showing his wings impression was sad. (And he was NOT allowed to get a new tunic.) Today the R.A.F. does not want to remember this punishment, and it was always kept as a hush-hush deal. The following is an article by James Campbell which appeared in *AIRMAIL* some time ago and should be most enlightening to the reader. This is factual and a problem we all had heard about, thought I believe more common in Bomber Command than in Fighter Command. I could be wrong of course, and it is my own opinion.

One morning I was told that I had been moved to instrument flight. The F/Cmd said, "Grab your helmet and chute an report to C Flight."

Balls, I thought, I'm going to the CO. I asked his adjutant for an interview.

The CO called me in and said, "What's your problem?"

I told him.

Uplands Station had at that time just adopted 401 Squadron, so he said. How would I like another month's leave?

"Good," I said. So I returned to Windsor (Essex) and pondered my position. The bloody was war still on, and I had just heard of Dick Audent and his five-in-one sortie victory. A great position I'm in, I thought.

Because of my interview at RCAF HQ London and the fact that I was not allowed to return to operations in the Western Theatre, I contacted the Army in London, Ontario, hoping to be accepted then posted to the U.K. where I could ask for a transfer to the RAF. I received rejection papers from the Canadian Army. I was not allowed to fight anymore. My actions behind the enemy lines put me in a spot that I would be shot if captured. By this time I had sent a telegram to HQ Ottawa asking for my release.

My intent had been to stay in the Air Force, but with all posts taken up by Air Force zombies who simply stayed in Canada and never dared overseas, there was no place for me. I was told that I did not fit in this Air Force, "Especially since you were a fighter pilot." This classed me, in their eyes, as wild and uncontrollable.

In April 1945 I took my log books to the recruiting unit of the U.S. Army Air Corps in Detroit. They liked what they saw in my log book and sent me to higher authority. It was decided that, provided I could get exit papers from Canada, I would be accepted within their organization to be shipped to the Far East immediately.

I returned to Essex to greet each mail delivery in anticipation of my exit papers from this country, each day hoping that I could roar over to Detroit and be on my way. Finally I received a letter from Canadian Mobilization Section which informed me that, because I was on Special Class E Reserve, I was allowed to be absent from Canada 10 hours per week.

Damn, I thought. Why? If I'm on reserve, why can't I rejoin any old squadron? And if not, why do they hold me? My entry into the U.S.A.F. was killed.

While in Detroit one day I dropped into the Mexican Embassy and questioned their recruiting procedure. Their answer was, "Sorry, senor, but you must be of Mexican birth."

To this I replied, "Give me a shot of your blood and I'll go native for you."

This didn't impress them at all.

So I was back where I started, completely at a loss of what to do. Finding civilian employment was no easier, as the general assessment was that a fighter pilot had to be a real squirrel.

Soon the Japs were bombed into surrender with the A-bomb. Then came the news that Hitler was trapped in his bunker and an armistice was to be signed.

What a stunning blow for me as I was totally dedicated to flying and to war activities. What the hell will I do now? I never ceased in my quest to return to the U.K. and the Forces and participate in some sort of action. My desires were not to be fulfilled until the Korean conflict. But that was years down the road. My prospects in 1945 were dismal.

While travelling by bus around Detroit, I overheard people speak of picking up food in Canada and that the prices were much lower. This fact stuck in my mind, along with a remark about how good the chickens were. On my way into Essex one afternoon I got off the bus near the chicken hatchery. Hearing the peeps and seeing the colored chicks, I ordered 500 of them to be delivered to my father's address. I was determined to become a chicken magnate with a herd of chickens.

Now my father lived in a small cottage with a backyard of 100 by 80 feet. To have this order of chicks arrive must have been wild. They had chickens everywhere — in the top of the garage, on the bottom, in the rear porch of the house, and even in the bathtub. My mother put the more feeble ones under a light, covered over, trying to save them from the cold. As I have previously mentioned, my father's sense of humor was nonexistent. I guess this episode touched him off. I really can't say what he said upon being invaded by chickens, because I had taken off to Sudbury at the time to visit Doc Bernie, having forgotten about my order.

When I arrived days later back at the chicken ranch, my Dad simply looked at me and said, "What the hell were you thinking of and how the hell do you think we are going to raise them?"

"Sorry, Joe" I said. "Guess I made an error."

I spoke to Steve Randall in Toronto and suggested a chicken fry. He said OK, and I promised to bring the chickens. I loaded a large grab sack with broilers, and

98 / A Knave Among Knights in their Spitfires

```
                                          CONFIDENTIAL
                                          C 17942

                    MEMORANDUM

                                          25 Jun 57.

        SASO

        Korean Operations
        17942 F/L (D) Hillings

        1       This officer desires to place his application on file for
        operational engagement in the Korean Theatre, in case of any existing
        or future requirements by the RCAF.

        2       This request is placed for the following reasons:

                (a) Because of his current flying practice and the operational
                    techniques in the RAF - Day Fighting Development Squadron.

                (b) This officer is, at present, up-to-date on most of the
                    day superiority tactics.

                (c) Because of the advanced type of jet fighters that would
                    now be employed, comparison figures, tactics and valuable
                    high altitude tracking assessing would be available.

        3       It is believed that both he and the RCAF would benefit from
        the operations and the experience to be gained in such a conflict.

                                          [signature]
                                          (D Hillings) F/L
                                          300ps/1
                                          (212)
```

The many " Memos ", to join a Squadron, etc. to no avail. No one bloody listening.??

Jerry on trails of a Mk. V Supermarine Swift, 1954. West Rayham, England, U. K.

took off via train to Toronto, ferry to the Toronto island, and handed Mrs. Randall the bag of chickens.

"OK," she said. "We'll have a good feed.".

I excused myself and visited the Royal York Hotel. I then decided to go to Montreal, and took the next train to that city. Steve told me later that they waited for hours for me and thought that perhaps I had been hurt or something. I really forgot about that dinner until I was about a half hour out of Toronto. By then, what could I do?

After a couple of days in Montreal I returned again to Windsor to figure out what I was going to do. Chicken farming was not for me.

In high school my main desire, after flying, had been to become a commercial artist. Seeing the advertised rehabilitation for veterans, I entered their office in Windsor to inquire about the possibilities of continuing in this field. When I was told that it would take three to four years of training, I left and spent a few hours in the bars in Detroit. I returned to the rehab office and asked them again to list the courses available.

Going down the list of carpenter, electrician, pharmacist, I came across cosmetologists. "Here", I said. "Sign me up for this one."

The guy raised his eyebrow and said, "Are you joking?"

"No". I said. "What's the matter? Can't I have it?"

"OK", he said.

In three days I received a letter and rail tickets for Toronto to start the course there. No one was more surprised than I when I entered a hairdressing school on Gerrard Street. If it hadn't been for the shapely maidens all around I might have retreated. But instead I stayed to participate. Why not? One of the shapely vivacious brunette instructors took me into her confidence and taught me well. Not only was I receiving extra instruction, but I was enjoying it as well. I completed the course. Fully qualified, I decided to open a shop of my own. I took with me three of the instructors of the school, one brunette, of course, one redhead and one blonde. We agreed that when the expenses were paid we would split the take four ways. Everything seemed to be going fine, and why shouldn't it with such a staff.

One day I heard a commotion in the reception room which was full of the best clientele. I entered the room and came face to face with none other than Goody Goodwin. He was dressed in his best blues, looking rather pleased, when he cried, "Jerry, what are you doing in here."

I said, "I'm sorry, sir. Can I assist you?"

"What the hell do you mean assist me," he said. "Ass me but don't ist me, old cock, where the Christ are the drinks?"

"I'm sorry, ladies". I said. "This gentleman is obviously confused. "Come, sir, in the back and I'll see if I can help you."

Pulling for all I was worth at the little Christer's sleeve, I finally got him into the back of the shop. There Goody said, "What the hell is going on and what is this place?"

"A cosmetologist empire." I replied.

He burst out laughing, and I said, "I gotta get out of here."

That night as I lay awake, I though over what Goody said, and the next morning I contacted a lawyer. I explained my position and said, "Get me out of this by noon if you can."

At precisely 11:15 he called and by 11:55 I was free and clear of the cosmetic nonsense. I hopped aboard the 2:30 train from Toronto to Windsor, leaving most of my belongings at the shop.

Here I might add that I was quite proficient as Helene Curtis in Chicago assessed me as the first class after a two-week stay.

As the train stopped at London, I recalled a place named Grand Bend, and I decided to visit the beach. After all it was only a few miles north, so why not? Arriving in the village I found a terrific beach with a large pavilion for recreation and dancing and a photographer's shop next door. I entered the photo shop and talked to the owner, who quite emphatically told me that a hairstyling shop was badly needed in the village. Next door was a vacant shop, ideally located, so I rented it, shipped the equipment from Toronto along with two of the operators and set up shop. Things went slow but steady.

On the beach they were having trouble locating a lifeguard. As I was seen continually on the beach, I was asked if I would be the lifeguard. Knowing full well that I could not swim but that the water was only knee keep for a good quarter mile out, I accepted the job.

For one month I held this post, hoping that I would never be called upon. At the end of the sixth week things got stale, so I departed Grand Bend as quickly as I had entered and finally made it back to Windsor.

A few weeks later I visited my hold high school principal, Pete Hall, and talked over my problem. He introduced me to Mac Brian at the Windsor Flying Club. He took me on as a chief flying instructor, a position I held for some eleven months.

Flying again was good, even in the old Tiger Moth.

On September 14, 1947 I won the coveted *Windsor Daily Star* Trophy in a race of 20 minutes 15 seconds for aircraft of 150 horsepower or less.

9. RE-ENLISTMENT 1948 RCAF

Some time around 1948 I had a telephone call from George Beurling, Canada's top fighter ace, who had in 1942 shot down several Eyties in Malta and explained his delight to see them destroyed in his book.[2] He told me of an Israeli group that was rounding up pilots to assist in the Israeli war. He and Leonard Cohen were scheduled to leave in a few weeks; was I interested.

Well, of course. Send me the information, I said. A brief note followed.

I was stunned to read the newspaper in May 1948 of his crash. He had stopped in Rome overnight on his way to the Israel/Palestine war. Why, I will never know But the next A.M. his aircraft burst into flames on takeoff, and he was burnt to death. He was flying a Norseman, an aircraft which to this day has never had that type of problem. Obvious to me, a direct act of sabotage. There was no investigation except by me much later, in 1962.

In mid 1948 I again applied to Ottawa for re-enlistment. At the end of the war Canada had the fourth largest air force in the world, but our French Prime Ministers did not press on, so they cut down on the aircraft, they cut down on the army. In September my old S/Cmd Johnson wrote to say that he was on the selection board and that he had seen my name. W/C Charles was head of the interviewing staff, which relieved me greatly, as he was someone I knew of from England where he had been a Squadron Commander during the war.

Old Jimmy "Shaky" Dew, a former Spitfire pilot from Flint, Michigan and I went together to Toronto and were immediately accepted. Shaky was killed in a Mustang at Winnipeg when his engine cut and he elected to stretch his glide to avoid houses.

I shook out the old uniform and proceeded to Centralia where I was soon checked by Dean Kelly in the Harvard. In three weeks I was off to Trenton to take an instructor course.

My first impression of this peacetime station wasn't too appetizing. A character by the name of Lasek pointed to my two rows of ribbons and said, "Don't think they are going to help you here, son. You've got to be good."

My intention was not to be good, but to be selected for a fighter squadron, as they had just gotten the jet Vampire fighter, and certainly not to stay here.

To my disgust I not only passed the bloody course, but was held on as staff at this peacetime central flying school to instruct pilots to become instructors For three years I pounded the skies in this guise with one consolation, that I not only flew the Harvard, but was current on the C45 twin trainer, Mitchell B25, Lancaster, Mustang and Vampire jet, and this wasn't hard to take. Generally in training command after the war you were lucky to fly one aircraft so here we were able to fly all these.

In 1950 I joined in a two-plane acrobatic team with Hal Knight to perform in airshows across the country in the Vampire jet. Though it never went to war the

---

[2] *Malta Spitfire*. New York: Farrar and Rinehart, 1943.

Vampire was very good for airshows. You were able to stay within the confines of the airport and on stage the whole time.

In 1951 the Canadian Jet Aero team was short a #2 in its formation. This team, of course, was commanded by Air Defense Command (ADC), while I was in Air Training Command (ATC). This created a problem. The chief personnel at ADC won out, and I was flown to St. Hubert, Quebec by F/L Bud Irving to join the team.

The team leader was a grumpy type who never really appreciated my presence, but to him I filled the gap, and he, in return, received excellent assessments as a leader. For me it broke my ties with training command.

Once the summer was finished I was posted to the Jet Operational Training Unit in New Brunswick in October 1951 to instruct young chaps to fly jets in Europe and Korea. Old Kelly, I found, had already arrived before me. He took me aside to introduce the T33 aircraft to me. I enjoyed Kelly's company again, only to see him posted shortly after to 411 Sabre jet Squadron and moved to Luffenham, England.

In March 1952 our first F86 Sabres arrived, and was I put in charge of first checking out the staff and then setting up the courses for F86 training. Here the cough drop twins — a pair of Smiths — were in control, W/C Flying W.J. Smith (Bill), and S/L E.G. Smith (Eric).

I enjoyed the stay here, flying with such characters as Sly Slyvester, Stu Wooley, Tom Wheeler, Jack Malone, Fritz Fitzgerald, Odie Levere, Larry Spurr, Bruce Fleming, Bob Hamilton, Doug Lindsay, Lowery, Howie Roe, Pappy Gibbs, Phil Etiene, Omar Lavesque, Petries, McMillan, and even old Larry Robillard., Danny and Andy Lambros, and Snake McGeogh were also present.

On the first of April 1954 I entered the ground school to meet the new course. Tucked away in the rear, chuckling to himself, was none other than Goody Goodwin. Christ, I thought. Here we go again.

I flew often with Goody, generally reacquainting him with procedures and tactics. It was good to be with him again after all the years of horsing around, to rump around upstairs, knowing that we could wax anyone's arse in any hassle we came upon.

Trenton was blessed with a great number of non-wearing "Canada Badges" personnel. Spit and polish excelled, and of course everyone stood about at attention, ensuring no wrong impression was being taken of each other at any time. Quit Goody enters the scene. If I have left the impression that Goody was of a non-military appearance, this is untrue, for Goody was a natural. His physique, manner, and natural style, with his two rows of ribbons (him being the top pilot to be honoured by the King for destroying the most enemy trains and transport in the Western Theatre), made him stand out in any group. But he was a heller.

Goody retired one evening and, on entering his bed, found that he had forgotten to turn the lights out, whereupon Goody took out his trusty .38 and blew them out.

Well. One can imagine the results. But really, in the modern age, I can agree with Goody. Why should anyone be obliged to turn a light off across the room and then chance your journey back to your pit in utter darkness. How many do this today?

Goody's stay was short, the course lasting for a matter of weeks, then their graduation and posting to Europe on a squadron of F86 Sabre jets.

In 1952 this group of O.T.U. pilots and instructors was almost comparable to the old squadron days, everyone overly keen to fly, but after flying there was nothing to do in New Brunswick but go to the mess and drink beer. Three of the guys, really burly types like football players, would wrestle in the middle of the anteroom floor. They had the appearance of bear cubs pawing around, each trying to hold the other down. It was in one of these episodes that I observed Neil Burns trying to make Bob Clark say uncle, as he had a twisting grip on an ankle which he thought was Bob's but the ankle in fact belonged to Tiny Thompson. Bob simply lay smiling at Neil, while Thompson was screaming bloody murder. We had to intervene or else Thomson's ankle would have been broken.

On another quiet evening while our station doctor, a Scotsman who enjoyed gin and tonic, was beating out a tune on the piano, Odie Levere proceeded to the lav where he found Larry Spurr lying on the floor. Odie nudged Larry Spurr with his foot to stir him, when at that moment, Al Perry entered, grabbed all 108 pounds of the 5 foot 2 inch Odie by the collar and pants, and threw him out of the door. Odie went headlong into the corner of the door jam, splitting his head open one or two inches at the top. He slumped to the rug, rather dazed.

Neil entered at this moment, and, being a close buddy of Odie, nailed Perry full in the eye with his mammoth fist. Perry departed for home. However, half way there, he thought, "He can't do that to me. I'm going back and nail that so and so."

Perry returned and tapped Neil on the shoulder. Neil wheeled immediately and nailed him in the other eye.

Old Perry had to leave the next day on temporary assignment to Montreal along with two black eyes.

Actually Neil and Perry were close friends.

As all of this was happening I summoned the doc from his gin and piano, and said, "We got a stitching job to do on Odie Levere. Come on."

We took Odie to the infirmary, and the doc proceeded to stitch. After the first stitch, with Odie sitting there groaning and cursing, the doc said to me, "Would you like to try one?" (The doc was a hell of a fine chap and one of the boys.)

I said, "Yeah give me the needle." And I applied the second stitch.

Larry Spurr, the dog who created all this, was now leghorne again and watching all of this. He peeped up and said, "Hey you guys, wait. It's my turn." And took command of the needle. Spurr's entry was a little too deep, so doc said, "O K, lads, let me finish so we can return to the mess."

Tiny Thompson was killed a few months later in a Sabre jet. He took off to do a weather test and went straight in. He had just bought a new hat and the local clothing supply guy downtown in Chatham was really upset — who was going to pay for this hat now? So we had to take up a collection. Money was a problem.

Odie survived until 1956, when he was checking out a Yankee chap in a T33, doing aerobatics, and his wing folded, came over the cockpit and they were trapped.

Larry Spurr was one of the first RCAF pilots to fly in the Korean War, where he shot down a couple Migs, then came back to the O.T.U. He retired in 1973. About the first month he was retried, as he was driving on the highway in, Nova Scotia, he came over a hill to meet an oncoming car driving on the wrong side. Larry was killed in the head-on collision.

Still another episode at the mess involved Bill Gould, a native of Fredericton, New Brunswick, a real swell, likeable chap, always smiling. He had the ability of a leopard, swift in movements with strength to match. He became the pacifier — or cock of the walk, so to speak. As old Ian McMillan would say, "Yes, Bill will ensure that everything shall be in order."

On New Year's Day, while we were all run down from the night before and sitting around the anteroom, we were startled to see the cook, a real masculine type, standing in the door of the dining room, wearing only his shorts and beating his chest, saying, "I can take on anybody in the mess."

Uncle Billy stood up, taking his tie and shirt off, saying, "Oh no, this is too good to be true." He stripped to his shorts, took a few catlike steps toward the cook — who was heavier and a good ten inches taller — grasped him, raised him over his head and threw him to the floor.

Furious, the cook got up and charged at Bill, who threw him down again. Three times Bill repeated this procedure, whereupon the cook departed into the kitchen and broke every dish and cup in the place. It was quite wild. The police came and removed him to the psycho ward in the local hospital. Because of this episode the C/O ruled that we all should be assessed to replace the broken dishes.

In the six years I spent at the OTU I participated in the teaching of aerial combat to some 90 courses of pilots, each having 30 pilots.

The cough drop twins finally rescued me. On the 10th of June 1954 they called me aside and said, "How would you like to go to England?" "Wow", I thought, "would I?"

My tour was to be as an exchange officer with the RAF (my pride and joy), in their Fighter Development Squadron to fly as a test and evaluation pilot on Britain's new fighter jets, the Hawker Hunter and the Supermarine Swift. What a posting, again to be free to enjoy the good old English countryside.

Keen to get going again, I hustled to pack. Upon arrival I was greeted by a Britisher, Stan Hubbard, who immediately took me under his wing and showed me the aircraft and the local ropes. In less than ten days I had flown the Meteor Mk 7 and 9, the Vampire, Sabre V, the Canberra with F/O Green from Bingbrook, the Hunter I, the Venom (which is a suped-up Vampire), Anson (a lumbering old thing we used to take a bunch of guys up and teach them navigation), and the Chipmunk. I made it a point to fly everything they had. This is one thing a pilot is not allowed to do in Canada. You have the chairborne people in Canada; they don't really get air under their butt. They like to draw up rules and regulations. So if you were in an area where there were other aircraft, you were probably allowed to fly the one and they wouldn't let you fly more than one.

A/C Bird Wilson was the C/O. Others were Ellecombe, Des Shean, Al Woodcock, Bob Broad, McElhew, Martin Chandler, Withy Blair, Dave Rhodes and Tony Carver.

Weekends found me roaring off either in a T33 or F86 from North Luffenham and the RCAF 411 Squadron where Dean Kelly was in charge and able to arrange the aircraft for these excursions. Duke Warren was the O.C., a most agreeable chap and one that could recognize a pilot's ability immediately. Kelly and I would invariably fly to Baden Baden, Germany on the Rhine and enjoy the German hospitality.

One day we had ordered eight cases of Boch beer to take back with us to the U.K. We had a T33. When the ground crew saw us with the loot, they asked where we were going to put it all. We loaded the nose completely and then, leaving our ejection pins in our seats, said, "Hand us the bottles." Each of our cockpits was piled with bottles of beer, but one case remained. I said, "Fire it up, Kelly, and I'll hold the case in my lap". Had we crashed, the investigation team would never have been able to answer that scene.

Over Holland, Kelly, being nature minded, began weaving and rolling about saying, "Look at all those tulips."

"Kelly, remember the case I'm holding. Will you stop pulling G's? You're breaking my arms.

On arrival at Rayham, UK we checked the signal area which clearly showed that the aerodrome was not shut down, so we landed. I was just completing the buttoning up of the nose area as Kelly sat inside with the engines running for a quick departure, when I noticed a car coming toward us. It was A/Cmd Grandy, later to become Air Chief Marshall of the RAF. He pulled up and said, "Billing, what are you doing here?" That question again. "You know the aerodrome is closed on weekends?"

"Yes, sir", I said. "But the signal area is clear and we thought today was an exception."

"Yes, is that right? Well, take your loot and get out of here quickly."

I turned to Kelly, have him a wink and departed. Kelly had his wheels tucked up shortly after for North Luffenham.

About this time, breaking the sound barrier by the Canadian pilots in their F86 Sabre jets aimed at the HQ at Luffenham, UK was beginning to be a problem. Old Red Summerville the CO, told his pilots that the next one to do this would be fired. Kelly advised me of this notice, so I promptly fired up a Hawker Hunter, roared towards Luffenham, and from 38,000 feet rolled vertically down, gun sight on Luffenham's HQ and went through Mach One. Each day for the next week I carried out the same exercise. On the next Monday I was headed for Luffenham when I noticed four F86's patrolling over the area. I carried on, and upon reaching the aerodrome, half rolled through Mach One, then dive brakes out, throttle off, and went in for a pitch and landing.

I taxied to Kelly's flight and found him walking out. I told him what I had done, and as usual old Kelly laughed, rubbing his right earlobe, saying, "Good, good. It's a lot of nonsense anyway. How about Baden, Friday?"

"OK, Kelly, call me. But why not try for Copenhagen, OK?"

On the 16th of September 1954 I was in a section of three Hunter jets doing close pansy formation for the photographers of the British magazine *Aeroplane*. We completed the exercise and returned for landing. I was flying #3 position. We all broke overhead and positioned ourselves for landing. For some reason I had a faulty gear indicator, and my port landing gear collapsed on landing. Damn, I though, a new fighter and me in the first prang.

The senior tech officer, W/C Bronsson frowned when I gave my report, failing to see how it could happen. G/Cpt. Rosie's comments were, "Whether one accepts the evidence of the pilot or not, at this time I see no reason to disbelieve his statement that three greens were showing."

He continued to say that since this accident, a Hunter aircraft from A and A E E had belly landed because of port undercarriage problem.

Here is where the statement of A/C Bird Wilson qualifies the trust, loyalty and faith in a fighter pilot to fighter pilot. His statement on the report of Hunter Mk I W.T. 588-16-9 54 which I still have copies of says: "Billing states his green lights were all showing. I have no doubt about it." And why not? If I had made an error, what really did I have to loose by trying to cover up, and certainly I would have stated my error, if I had made one. Bird Wilson knew this fact as well as I did.

My two years to the RAF on exchange posting gave me valuable experience. Perhaps too much, as I was returned to Canada to spend time at a desk (Defense Command, Montreal). This to me was absolutely appalling. In the RAF I could be flying next to the station commander on many occasions, as the RAF hold to and has always maintained flying status. This did not go unrecognized in the RCAF, because they introduced a rule that flying pay would not be automatic, and log books must be stamped and signed against a set number of flying hours per quarter. This was a try — and the aircrew to come out of the woodwork when the order was introduced was startling — but it simply led to sharp-pencilling and created the situation where it made officers bend the truth. I saw pilots who were now seeking a career (to hell with flying), enter one hour thirty minutes or one hour forty-five minutes on the log and only fly thirty minutes. Because "their" paper war was endless, they invariably were the ones to be promoted. Rather sickening, but a fact.

I was placed on the flight test subcommittee of the great Canadian Avro Arrow jet, and attended meetings in Toronto. Every meeting the first thing on the agenda was the need for more money to complete the building of this aircraft. Here we had an aircraft hull — or hulk — with a borrowed engine. It had no fire-control system. Hughes Co. told us they could not entertain the contract for the fire control system installation, as they had too many other U.S. projects pending. RCA was approached and given the contract even though they had never seen the aircraft.

No weapon was available to put on this aircraft with its mystic fire control system.

The 'great' Canadian Iroquois engine was to be the source of energy for this great aircraft which was to prove Canada ahead of the world in aircraft design, but the bloody engine was blowing up at 87% heat trails in the U.S.A. This so called fantastic engine, without all this supposed potential, never flew in any aircraft or was sold to any country.

When I returned to Air Defence HQ, Montreal I wrote a full report and asked to be taken off this committee. I believed the Avro Arrow was going no where. This did not sit well with the paper merchants and did very little for my advancement in the RCAF. Some months later Canada's Prime Minister, Mr. Diefenbaker (at the urging of his advisors, not his decision) cancelled the Avro programme — to me an extremely wise move and the saving of millions of tax dollars.

I had just returned from the UK on an exchange programme where the British had drawers full of plans for aircraft as good or better than the Arrow. My problem, being just a F/Lt. was that I expressed my views too clearly.

The wheels were yes men who went along with any armchair advisor, not like the RAF men who always got air under their arse before making decisions. One also must remember that amongst the RCAF were admirable gentlemen, but also they were handicapped by as foul a collection of overpaid bureaucrats as exists in this world.

I was also on the cockpit modification committee of the Canadian CF100 jet, but had never flown one. When I asked the character in charge for me to get checked out on it, he became hostile. Because of his attitude and lack of reasoning, I simply proceeded to the CF100 unit, told the O.C. of my problem, and he immediately gave me CF100 time. When the other mulehead from HQ found this out, he was speechless. This also did not help my career.

When my instrument qualifying ride was upon me, old Lorne Tapp gave me the necessary long-pencilled ride. Lorne was a pilot from way back, being one of the heroes of the Berlin Air Lift. Lorne for some reason was selected to be a test pilot in Montreal on the Mach I CF104 aircraft. He told me of his first flight, that the tower had asked him if he was ever going to take off as he was holding on the active runway. He replied, "Yes, I'm going to as soon as I can get my feet to come off the brakes."

Lorne's definition of acceleration is: "When it drags your foreskin back, that's acceleration. Those being circumcised won't appreciate this feeling."

The continuing paper war was getting to me. Writing interoffice memos etc., to have them returned by higher ups, bleeding to death with red ink corrections in their never-ending quest to produce empires within empires was not only time-consuming but extremely costly to the public. One particular report I remember clearly was to write a staff paper on the requirements of a hunting knife as part of a pilot's survival gear.

Firstly one must start off and explain a knife, then the different types of knives, and then introduce the knife of which you are speaking. With all of this conjunctive clauses/split infinitives/dangling participles nonsense, and because my eyes were beginning to bleed from the professor-like corrections, I entered the archives of Defense Command in the basement, hoping to come up with the original report of this bloody knife. Hell, we had been issued it years ago, and someone must have written something.

It took me over an hour to find what I was looking for, but there it was, and I'll be damned, it had been written (plus rewritten) only recently. I signed out the necessary paper and took it to the secretarial pool — which was a sight to behold in itself, consisting of not only shapely beauties, but one hell of a lot of them.

Having completed this staff paper again in draft, I waited a couple of days, then submitted this study, supposedly drawn up by myself, to the very person who had originally constructed it.

I waited. I wasn't long before it came back across my desk bleeding to death, with an attached note to the effect that he had never quite seen such a mess.

With the original in hand, I entered his presence and compare my staff paper to the one with his name on it — I thought proving a point. As he was senior to me, the point I proved was almost fatal.

It did, however, I'm sure save me from the ill-fated desk-bound group, but set back any immediate advancement anywhere. Small mind, I thought. Why couldn't facts be accepted? I really wasn't quite ready to hang up my helmet and rot behind an inkwell.

While in the Defence Command as a pencil pusher, I had flown such types as the C45, C47, T33, F86, CF100, and am pleased to say that my monthly actual air time was as much as I have ever flown when I was on full flying duties. Every weekend found me aloft in a T33.

In all, one of the saddest things to record that I found from my re-enlistment in 1948 until I finally retired was the drastic change in over fifty percent of the aircrew's attitude. Subservience, which I detest, became a way of life for a great many pilots, and their effort to plan their careers by this method, pushing aside the act of flying, was to me most distressing.

Old Buck NcNair told me in 1950, "Jerry, I know well what you see, and believe me I suggest, if you really want to get ahead in this air force today is, when you go flying, walk out to your aircraft, put your chute down, shit on the tail, and go back to the desk." This, coming from one of Canada's top air aces, summarized the top brass's thinking throughout the system.

Some of the better types at ADC were such characters as old Don Norman, Jack Dunstan, Tapp, Phil Etiene, and W/C Bob Braham, DSO and 2 bars, DFC and 2 bars, AFC, the most decorated aerial killer of the RAF who had only recently transferred to the RCAF. Bob was a terrific man and was the type that one could talk to regardless of rank or seniority.

At lunch one day we were discussing the promotion structure. Bob had just returned from Ottawa HQ from an interview regarding his standing for promotion. The senior official reviewing his personnel record summarized the interview with, "I'm sorry, Bob, but your lack of education is a problem."

Bob's remark to this was "Hitler never asked me how much education I had."

How bloody true.

Bob was to come to my rescue later. I was stationed in New Brunswick, and on Friday evenings I would fire off to Trenton, Ontario in a T33 jet, board the air transport for Marville, France, hop aboard a train to Spain for a day, get back in time to reboard a train, transport back to Canada to arrive back in New Brunswick on Monday morning at 6 o'clock, shave and be ready for air work at the flight. No one within the RCAF really knew where I was. My personal contact with the many pilots I had trained enabled me to arrange the flights. My excursions from New Brunswick to Europe on weekends became so frequent that pilots on squadrons at Marville and Gros Tanquin thought I was actually stationed in France. Other than visit Spain, I would borrow a T33 jet in France and roar off to Copenhagen for a day.

On one of these trips I became quite ill (I'm sure someone fed me a mickey) travelling to Spain by train. I immediately got off and took a taxi to the nearest hotel. I called my buddy, Jean Lebreton in Paris and told him of my illness. The hotel proprietor was most helpful and assisted me in obtaining medicine and train travel back to Paris, where I was taken care of by John's wife Marthe.

I was violently ill, extremely weak and perspiring. My position now was of being not only ill, but out of the country with only a few hours remaining to catch my flight back to Canada.

I called Bob Bramliam, who was at that time Air Attaché in Paris, and told him of my position and problem.

"Don't worry, Jerry. I'll have my staff car around immediately and set everything up." Which he did.

Once back in Canada, I could report ill with no problem.

Bob Braham died of cancer at age 53, a great loss to everyone.

On another of these trips to France I contacted Errol Flynn, who I had met in Los Angeles during the years that I was on civy street after World War II. He was a likeable chap but inclined to be a bit of a heller. I should like to have seen old Goody and him in operation. The last I heard from him was when I was in France on one of my excursions and I sent a cable to him in the Nice area. I was invited down to spend a few days on his yacht but my tight schedule prohibited it. My comments when he died were, "The King is dead."

Chicago - Len Boose.....Checking the Rolls Royce Engine after the second stage blower turbine left its shaft

10. JET TACTICS AND WEAPONS UNIT & 129 TEST AND FERRY UNIT

I finally departed the paper war from Command HQ and arrived at Chatham, New Brunswick OTU. and on the 15th of March 1958 was given a unit checkout by F/L W.A.C. Wilson. My status was now over six years as a F/Lt. receiving progressive pay.

To bring me abreast with the weapons on the jet Sabre F86 I took the instructors' course that was presently run by Ernie Glover, who had flown in Korea. On my completion of the course, MacKenzie (who had been shot down in Korea, I'm sure by his Number 2, and became a prisoner of war) suggested that I forget the Weapons Unit, as he wanted me to run the Tactical Squadron. For me this would mean more fun and longer trips, as the Weapons Unit were not equipped with drop tanks.

Shortly after arriving I was posted to a survival course for one week in the foothills of the Rockies. This, I thought, was all I need — survival.

The course consisted of nothing more than building an outdoor shelter to sleep in the open for six days. A fat S/Ldr in charge of the course capitalized by selling homemade flint lighters to everyone on the course, and that is about the only significance that I have to record about that.

Air shows were quite common, and I found myself leading sections of jet Sabres to thrill the girls and thousands who turned out for air displays in St. Hubert, Moncton, Greenwood, Ottawa, and numerous cities or airports requested them.

My continued urge to join a squadron was always present. I ran the tactics flight with characters like Larry Spurr, Fitzgerald, Yvon Hallee, John Farnham, Jack Mulhall, Jebb Kerr, Lloyd Hubbard (a fine type to whom I gave his first roll in formation). Lloyd later on became leader of the Golden Hawks aerobatics team. On 10 August 1959, Jebb was killed after completing an, overshoot in one of the Golden Hawks aerobatics Sabres to have a midair with a light aircraft.

One of the great problems we had was teaching the Greek and Turkish pilots sent over for squadron training. They had great problems with the language (or we had), and on one occasion, while sitting on the runway as a section of two, trying to establish radio contact with a Turk, I pointed to his helmet, whereupon he took it off, turned it around backwards, and gave the thumbs up, OK?

On another occasion, the surface wind gave indication of shifting, which would mean landing on a shorter runway. I briefed the group on the problems — speed, height, etc. — and on landing found that one of the group had simply set his speed or height and flew directly into the hydro wires on the approach end. He said, "They were in the way, Sir."

We also trained German Airforce pilots, some being from World War II era. I had wanted to now to advance and join some unit with a more powerful aircraft. I visited Dow Airforce Base of the U.S.A. to beg for a ride in the century series jet. A captain Bill Grunzebocht took me aloft in a Voodoo F101 jet to experience doing in and out of the speed of sound.

Flying with the Germans, I continually questioned them on the type and status of their new fighters. They were to receive the Mach one CF104 Shooting Star, and soon. A Lt. Herbst was on the course, and I asked him if he would like to go to Montreal for a trip in a T33 jet trainer. Of course, I told him, it would mean penetrating the U.S. border en route. I built up a good case whereby we would be illegal and would fly by the Nike rocket site at Presque Isle, Maine, and we would be low level so that the radar could not detect our presence. By the time we were ready to press tits he was ecstatic. Our trip did indeed follow the planned route, and one hour and twenty minutes later, we lowered our gear to land in Montreal. He was most impressed that we had gotten through undetected and made quite a fuss once we returned to his group.

By mid 1960 it was quite apparent to me that I would never be posted to a squadron. I had squashed my chances of promotion and two-year posting to Oldenburg, Germany exchange with the German Airforce. Recalled suggesting that I stay in Canada. This cheesed me so much that on 7 June 1960 I flew with John Farnam to Ottawa for an interview with the German Airforce. The Germans were most impressed with my qualifications, but the language was a problem. I assured them that I could learn to speak the language and they agreed. However, because I would eventually end up in a ground position, writing of the language would be a detriment. I was not accepted.

How would my father have taken my enlisting in the Luftwaffe?

For the next two years I continued flying in the tactical role, and by now I had passed a record of being 20 years as a combat ready fighter pilot. Each year had the inevitable airshows, including National Exhibition shows, which incidentally I have flown in fourteen times in various types of aircraft.

Off days at the O.T.U. would find me on the Miramichi River, catching salmon with Fred Murdock and Gene Galland, local natives that I had gotten to know and with whom I became close friend.

I remained at the Ops training unit until 22 May 1962, when I was posted to Trenton, Ontario again, to join the 129 Test and Ferry Unit.

Leaving New Brunswick in May 1962 for Ontario never bothered me too much, although I had run into personal problems especially with a chairborne artist who was the C.O., and the type who had remained at Trenton throughout he war. Here I was able to fly the C45, C47, T33, F86, CF100 jet, along with the Albatross, Chipmunk, Otter, Lancaster and Mitchell North Star. My job here really was nothing more than to test aircraft from retrofit and deliver them to RCAF bases across Canada.]

Old Dad Thompson, Jim Fewell, Don Norman, Tex Wheatherly, Chris Frost, Tim Martin, Mulrooney, and Kettles were most of the gang at the unit. J. Fewell was our C.O., who actually preferred golf at that time to the problem of becoming airborne.

Chris Frost, a George Medal winner, was the chap that I more or less teamed up with. If I required to be picked up, Chris would be the one volunteering.

In June we were delivering T33 jets to France. Canada had given C45, T33, and C47 aircraft to that country for aid. Our trip to France took us via Goose Bay,

Greenland, Iceland and Scotland to Europe. We were dressed in rubber dunk suits, good for all of fifteen minutes in the cold arctic waters, if obliged to bail out. I made four of these trips and each one was without incident. In Greenland I loaded down the jet with $1.50 40 oz. bottles of Scotch to give to an old retired colonel at "The Priory" on Lake of Monteith, Scotland. We always had a two days stop here. The story goes that Mary, Queen of Scots, was beheaded in that area and at times she rises from the mist out of the lake. I'm sure I've seen her several times.

In 1962 I had completed 20 years as a fighter pilot, still going strong. My main desire however, never materialized, and that was to join a fighter squadron again. The air force kept me on fighter tactical and weapons training throughout.

In November, en route to India in an old Dakota aircraft, Dad Thompson and I stopped in Rome for two days. While there I suggested we visit City Hall to seek out information regarding George Beurling. We found the right man, who told us that the records normally stay intact for some 15 years. They stay in the office on the main floor for ten years, then are put in the basement. I asked who decided this. He informed me that that was the procedure.

Being in uniform, I informed him that I had been instructed to notify the appropriate authorities to have the records remain on the main floor until notified and that I would sign any papers necessary for that request. If you visit Rome you will find that the records are still available on the main floor.

It was interesting to note that although George had been buried in the old Protestant Cemetery in Rome, the good Israeli people moved his body, which now rests in Tel Aviv, Israel. A terrific gesture, I thought. In Canada, at the time of his death, there was a brief headline in the newspaper for a day, then the book closed.

While in Rome, old Dad Thompson and I ankled through the streets once trod by the Gladiators. Today, as you know, the great Coliseum is plagued with many house cats going wild to roam at will. One day we entered the Coliseum and, before I knew what was going on, I heard the screams of cats and the cursing of old Tommy. When I located him, I found him with a long stick, having two house cats cornered.

I said, "Thompson, what in hell are you doing?"

"I'm re-enacting the fight of the gladiators. Stand back!"

After doing battle with the cats, Tommy's next episode was to enter the Fountain De Trevi to fill an empty wine container with water to bring back to Canada. The local Gestapo put a stop to this. They had to drag Thompson, who was ankle deep in the spilling water, from the Trevi scene.

Later on, we were having some difficulty getting a table in a local restaurant, as seating was at a premium. Since Thompson looked like Al Capone, I eased over to the Maitre, and in a low voice said," Please don't upset him, he is Capone's number 3 man." We were immediately seated and the service supreme. I expressed our thanks as we departed, with old Thompson growling, "What the hell's going on? What's da matter wid dose guys"? Typical of him.

11. TEST PILOTS, DEHAVILLAND CANADA VIETNAM 1965 - 1966

I have always had a great problem just trying to remain flying. Always someone or some bloody order to stop or stay on the ground comes along. Such was my compulsory retirement from the RCAF in 1964. The 500 pilots that were fired in 1965 proved fatal to the air arm of Canada. It never recovered. Six months later a cry went out: We are short of pilots. By 1988 pilots were leaving the service at a critical rate to join the commercial airlines. One cannot blame them for that. In 1943 I flew with a chap who quit the RCAF and the war to join a major airline to eventually be paid over $100,000 a year and retire at some $ 3,500 a month. I stayed on in the air arm to be paid some $10,000 a year and retire at $850 a month, and fight like hell to remain a fighter pilot.

Leaving the RCAF under their cut back programme has never really impressed me nor did the wheels who planned the scheme, but it was great to be with a select group again as a test pilot at DeHavilland in Toronto along with George Neal, Dave Fairbanks, Mick Saunders, Bob Fowler, Colin Phillip, and Arny Holingsworth. We had a terrific staff in Buck Buchanan, George Hern, Henry Jones and John Shaw. I was engaged in the test trails of the turbo prop driven Buffalo aircraft, a STOL type that could handle tons of payload easily. Flying mainly with Bob Fowler and Mick Saunders, these trials continued for the Canadian and U.S. governments for production of this machine for the forces. The company also had a four-engined Heron Executive aircraft that I accompanied Dave Fairbanks in for special trips around the country.

Dave "Foo" Fairbanks was a fighter pilot in World War II flying mostly Tempest aircraft. He was a native of Ithaca, New York, and joined the RCAF in 1941. Dave flew all of his operations on RAF squadron, and was most successful, destroying more than 16 enemy aircraft. The Queen awarded him two bars to his Distinguished Flying Cross, an honour bestowed only on four other RCAF pilots. Dave was shot down after engaging 40-plus enemy aircraft and was taken prisoner of war, liberated after D-Day. I had known Dave for years and it was a delight to fly and ankle with him throughout the globe in many exotic adventures. Whenever we reached the halfway point around the world, Dave always drenched his hat in gas, lit it, and would do an Indian war dance around it, toe to heel, hell to toe type, always to the delight of the natives watching. (Dave died in Toronto 20 February 1975. Bloody heart gave out. My son Brick has his watch.)

Dave and I took a Caribou aircraft to the Alaska panhandle for demonstration purposes to show how quick and simple it was to fly from the valley and village of Stewart, B.C. to the ice cap of Portal, about 25 kilometers northwest of Stewart and some 7,800 feet up the mountain. Someone, somehow found copper in the bloody mountain and the project was on. Time of course being of the essence, an aircraft was thought of. Caterpillar tractors took two days for the same trip that we took 15 minutes to do.

To impress the heavily clothed workers on the ice cap, I wore sole rubber and ea muffs. Dave had rubbers, a top hat and ear muffs. All I can say is thank God our engines started, for I'm sure they'd have said, "OK, smartasses, freeze."

We were able to do six trips to the ice cap, hauling all types of cargo before the snow came, and then we agreed that the demonstration was complete. On each approach to the ice cap, circling around the south side of the mountain and the camp, I had mentioned to Dave about the colour, greenish white, and wetness of the whole camp. We both agreed that to us it looked too hairy to live on. Our feelings were confirmed two weeks after our departure when the bloody ice cap shifted and several men were killed.

The Vietnam war of course was on and the CIA, through various agencies, purchased aircraft from Canada. Each year we delivered a Caribou from the factory, with U.S. markings, to Saigon. Our route was via the Azores Islands, Spain, the Isle of Rhodes, Damascus, Sharjah, Calcutta and Bangkok, to Vietnam. While taken the DeHavilland Caribou aircraft to Vietnam, old Dave Fairbanks and I were able to visit many out of the way places around the world. We landed in Rhodes, the isle of roses, a Greek island south of Turkey for a layover. The Colossus of Rhodes was one of the seven wonders of the world, a giant of a man standing with his legs astride the harbour entrance on two pillars. The ships of ancient times used to sail into the harbour between his legs, so large was the statue, which today does not stand, although the pillars are still in place.

The island is the very spot where all the exotic bases for perfumes of Paris come from. When the roses are in bloom the isle is covered in a bright blood color, absolutely beautiful. I would buy perfume from a large vat with a spigot, similar to those holding vinegar in North America. The fish taken from the Mediterranean Sea are fantastic and the most scrumptious that I have ever eaten. One can catch octopi as easily as dragging a trout in a well-stocked lake.

On one trip, as we were trying to fly to Rhodes, the weather became impossible. I was flying the beast while old Foo was trying to navigate. I could see the huge billowing clouds ahead of us and decided to race for an opening. The winds were increasing and whitecaps visible in the fading light of day. We continued, then everything closed around us, and suddenly, Wham! a hell of a noise broke out and I thought we had run smack into a hill. Large smashes hit the windscreen, as large as tennis balls, which I immediately recognized as hail. We were absolutely trapped, no prewarning, nor radar of course, nothing but charts and a radio compass.

"Dave, I'm turning north. See if you can contact the bloody Greeks — Athenia Control to get some weather somewhere."

We both began to get wet palms by now and found our work cut out for us. I wrestled with the aircraft while Dave began searching radio frequencies, trying to talk to someone. I took the navigation chart and began cross-checking for somewhere to land. We had departed the Isle of Majorca, Spain, hours ago and knew that continuation ahead was impossible — weather briefing again wrong. (I have always believed that weather forecasting is the only job anyone can have and be continually wrong and yet get a raise in pay.) I spotted a drome on the heel of Sicily and set course, while Dave was plotting cocked hats for our position. In driving rain and wild winds I wrestled the bloody aircraft for an instrument approach and landing. What a fight. Seeing the runway light, I pinned the Caribou on the runway while old Food was screaming on the radio: "You bloody Eyties can't you understand English. Clear the Goddamned area, we're coming in. Where the hell is your radar and get that so and so weatherman off his ass."

I was positive that when we left the aircraft and walked into the terminal, handcuffs and chain certainly would be waiting for us. To my surprise everyone stood up, moved back and treated us with a terrific deference. The next A.M. we looked at our machine. All leading edges were pock marked, resembling the finish of a golf ball. Foo said, "For —— sake, we might as well stay in Vietnam. We'll be shot and fired at for sure. Look at those dents. Oh no, what are we going to do?"

"Dave," I said "Did you see that brunette at breakfast? Well, I'm sure she wants to meet me. Let's go and get some coffee."

"You bastard. OK, let's go."

For 3/4 of an hour Dave compiled message after message to send to "MOTH", our HQ. Not one of them seemed to do the job, so I said, "It's done, Dave. Nothing we could or can do can change it. Let's deliver the machine. Maybe at night no one will notice."

We agreed. Upon our arrival in Saigon the condition of the aircraft caused not the least bit of concern. In fact everyone said, "Ah, a new machine. Good." That was that.

Passing through Sharjah, Trucial, Oman at the bottom of the Persian Gulf, on these trips, we found to be absolutely terrible. It's desert, and the jackals run loose in the town. You don't go out of your house at night or the jackals will attack you.

On one refueling stop we found the natives were fixing a road near the terminal. I took Dave over with my camera and grabbed the shovel from one of the natives, got down in the hole and started to dig like mad in a terrific cloud of sand and dust, until I suddenly stopped and picked up a nugget of gold that I had got in Alaska and had palmed and dropped unnoticed. Even Dave appeared surprised, until he realized what I had done. Of course this created quite a stir, and as we departed, old Foo said, "Look at them. Lookit 'em dig, you rotten bastard."

Our arrival in Bombay, India was something else. I have never in my life seen such filth. People live in low dirty lean-tos that resemble pig sties. Photos show the area, but never contain the smell. I firmly believe that everyone, mainly those who live on the North American continent, should visit Bombay, New Delhi or Calcutta, if only for one day and see. No one will believe this way of life and no one can describe it, nor can any amount of pictures show it. It has to be seen and smelled to get the full impression. People simply are born here, live, and die in the street and the filth. They endeavor to roll or wrap themselves in jute bags or paper at night to sleep on the earth or beside the roads. If, in the morning, the body does not move, it is simply dumped on the first garbage wagon going by. Cups, saucers, knives and forks are unheard of. What more can I say. Go and see, and then try to describe your impressions.

Bangkok, Thailand is, by far, one of the most majestic places in the world. The people have that soft graceful way of life, seldom seen anywhere else. The fresh seafood is beyond description. The morning market, on water, is a sight to see, but one has to get up for the 5:00 A.M. opening. I joined a group of Thai beauties who were processing fish; all were slim figured, with small breasts, and beautiful features and long black shiny hair.

Remember that Thai girls for years dominated the Miss World Beauty Pageant, and one can sure see why. I dug into the vials of water and moving objects and grabbed a live morsel. I thrust it between my teeth and growled. Dave cried, "Billing, get the hell out of there and leave the girls alone."

My Thai audience was greatly delighted, each with a wide grin ear to ear, which showed the bright red tongue and teeth covered by the juice of the Beetle Nut, so commonly chewed in that area. It has a similar effect to drugs.

Saigon arrival was a bit more trying. We had to fly South from Bangkok to the 10 degree parallel, then take up a heading to intercept Point Caman. From here we would be intercepted by the U.S. combat planes and flew low level up the Mekong Delta. All of this was with radio silence and by the use of dead reckoning and the aid of a fluctuating radio compass. Several times we looked at each other as we flew low level over the Siam Gulf and said, "What the hell are we doing here?" — a phrase I shall never forget as long as I live, for it has been an outstanding question thrown at me endless times, "Jerry, what are you doing here?" And each time I duck my head and search for cover. 'What am I doing anyway,' I think.

I slept that night on the table in a single room, having lost the bed to Fairbanks' double-headed coin, but was unable to slumber long, because of the continuous bombardment of the enemy across the Saigon River. Troops, vehicles, bicycles, girls, dogs and everything were in the congested streets. How, why and where they were all going was quite a mystery. On three occasions we were narrowly missed by the bloody blasts sent over by the Viet Cong.

In order to get back to Canada, Canadian Pacific Airlines ran from Hong Kong to Canada only on certain days. We made sure we didn't get back into Hong Kong until we'd miss a flight or two so we'd get more time in Hong Kong. When I was there I met a guy in CAT, Civil Air Transport, which was a clandestine outfit supported by CIA. These guys were flying their aircraft behind the lines, and I took a trip with him.

That afternoon an American mercenary pilot was taking a trip in an old three-tailed type aircraft to land somewhere in Viet Cong area near DaNang. He asked if I'd like to go. And of course, "Why not?"

We tooled along in this vibrating, thundering time bomb on a northerly heading, following the river north to the small village of Stung Treng, took the starboard river for, passing Attopeu, and continued north entering the rolling hills and mountain area to come out of pass and view the South China Sea. From here we landed and were met by numerous personnel wearing different types of clothing. Within ten minutes the aircraft was unloaded, fired up and we were looking for the pass that would lead us to Attopeu and Saigon. The pilot was something to behold. He gave me the impression that he was sitting on a vibrating machine, but actually the guy was triggered up so much that he was a nervous wreak. Gold was plentiful in Saigon, and this guy not only had a gold bracelet, but he had a gold bracelet around each ankle, and at times he had two cigarettes lit, not really remembering where each one was or had been put down.

On the return trip he became very talkative and humorous, and by the time Saigon came into view, he was overjoyed, flourishing an around-the-world ticket with thirty days to enjoy.

He was renting an entire house in Saigon with two maids and a gardener. This garden produced some of the largest and most gorgeous orchids I'd ever seen. "Want the keys to the house"? he said. "I won't be using it for a while."

"No thanks, but where is CAT HQ?" I said, wishing to hear of my chance of joining this clandestine group. I was told that as a Canadian it was impossible to entertain any form of employment.

I left Saigon aboard the Mandarin jet for Hong Kong. The Mandarin jet is intrigue in itself. This was a clandestine 737 jet. The interior is finished in black, gold and red. Dragons and far east goddesses adorn the walls and drapes of the entire aircraft. Your seat is secluded and separated from each other mysterious occupant by a curtain. You are escorted to go out to the aircraft at different intervals, so you never knew who was on the damn aircraft. You never knew who might be seated only an length away in any direction. No loud voices could be heard, as every conversation was indeed a whisper. You simply produced credentials; there was a nod, and you were directed to your seat. The flight continued in this manner, and I peered out the window hoping that a Red Mig jet would not appear. Once abeam Hainan Island I began to forget the events behind me, and looked forward to Hong Kong and Kowloon.

We stayed at the Ambassador Hotel in Kowloon on the mainland. While eating, one could look across the harbour to the isle of Victoria where Hong Kong rests. My first visit to the bar in the Ambassador found me being measured for a suit by Rony Lee, a tailor, as I sipped Coke.

I has been told that unless you are sharp, you'll be sold cloth loaded with camel hair, which is itchy to wear.

On my original contact with Rony Lee I expressed up front my dislike of being cheated, showed him by CAT ticket, and said, "If you do, I'll be back." I had no problems. I stayed in contact with Rony Lee for many years after, as he produced excellent suits.

Hong Kong is completely surrounded by China on the west side and by open water on the east. The small isle of Macao is an easy visit from there, only 45 kilometers from Hong Kong, and is an island that holds much intrigue, mystery and entertainment. There is nothing that you cannot purchase here — even your Canadian passport with a different date — all at a price. Hong Kong and Kowloon in those times were places unequaled in the world.

While sitting at the bar in the Ambassador I was fitted twice by a shoe merchant, and the next day had a custom-made pair of shoes delivered to me. The suit took longer.

Dave had, of course, organized our trip so that we would arrive in Hong Kong in time to "just" miss the CP air connection to Toronto, causing a two-day layover in Hong Kong. Terrible thing to do, I thought.

When travelling to Hong Kong from Kowloon, one is obliged to hire a rickshaw or else walk to the ferry. Dave boarded his rickshaw, and here I insisted that my driver hop in that I'd pull. With some reluctance and much jabbering by the other rickshaw coolies sitting around, he boarded and sat down. I pulled alongside Dave who was shaking his head, saying, "Billing, for Christ sake, give the coolie back his richshaw."

I looked behind to see the coolie grinning like Cheshire cat. The numerous highly efficient British about turned their noses to the sky, muttering, "Bloody Americans."

Actually, pulling the rickshaw is quite an art. I watched the other coolie driver and saw him ease backwards in the handles, then hop up to ride and rest for a good 25 - 30 feet. I found the center of balance and simulated the coolie. It worked. Old Dave tried to stop his driver in order that he might try. He kept saying, "How can I stop this meathead? How come I can't have some fun?"

We arrived at the dock puffing, and with the rider in my rick still grinning away. This smile, however, vanished when I turned and put out my hand for the fare. I continued to insist, until I looked around at the gathering coolies, and I quickly paid for my trip as the rickshaw coolie.

My stay at DeHavilland lasted two years, and possibly would have been longer, but my pay was $500 a month gross, and I had to draw from my salary while travelling around the world in order to survive. My taxi fare to and from Malton/Downsview was OK'd, but no response from my interoffice memos on the problem of money for expenses.

Reluctantly I left DeHavilland, but I had expressed my concern and simply had to follow through. Dave, and his secretary, Wendy, talked to me seriously, trying the persuade me to stay. Russ Bannock, a Mosquito pilot who became head of DeHavilland in Toronto after the war, guaranteed employment as long as I wished. However.

12. SPITFIRES

At the last of the war, the Supermarine company made a handful of eight dual Spitfires for the Irish air force. A millionaire in Windsor bought one of these dual Spitfires and wanted me to give him dual instruction. He was not a very good pilot.

We spent day after day practicing endless loops, doing the same thing over and over. This man's coordination was something else. He was never at ease when flying. On take off and landings he was quite tensed up.

After hours of rolls and ground briefing, he had yet to be able to hold the stick over in a roll, had no idea of coordination, to fly a numbers manoeuver. Many hours of ground briefing could not impart to the man the need for *respect* for the machine and not contempt.

A flight to remember:

We are ready to go. Start up incomplete and fuel gushing from under the starboard wing. I have extreme difficulty trying to warn everyone and especially to get him to turn off the battery switch. Finally he does.

The machine is fixed (fuel leak), and we are ready again. I can transmit, but I cannot receive. The radio merchant is reluctant to accept my suggestion on R/T and wiring for my oxygen mask. So we press on, slight run up and the front cockpit questions about going without my receiver. I said, "I'm OK. Everything checks good. Let's go. I can tell you if anything goes wrong."

Take off. No problem. I have no brake handle, so I plant my feet firmly in a position where he cannot over control. We are airborne, 400 feet, and he finally selects UP. Green light glows for the up selection. I am obliged to reduce power. What is he doing up front? No attempt to trim out the excessive rudder trim. But I can see he is really using the radio.

Finally at 2200 feet, I say, "Give it to me and I'll trim it out." At this point he is simply riding and hasn't touched any trim. I wind off rudder trim, ease off power, and trim out for cruise power straight and level. Beautiful. I then say, "OK, you have it now. It sure trims up terrific." (After we land I found that he had immediately contacted the engineer on our air/ground frequency and was panicking because he could not fly the aircraft and the trim and rigging was way off.) He was at that point most concerned, but settled down once I gave him control and trimmed out.

I again took control and climbed to 5000 feet, executed medium and steep turns, and stalled the aircraft clean and dirty (64 clean and 58 dirty), good for our return circuit and landing.

I then did a few rolls right and left, throttled right off and dived, climbed steeply, rolled to the inverted and allowed the nose to drop from a 45 degree above the horizon to a 45 degree below the horizon attitude while still inverted, rolled out, still with the throttle off, and descended steeply, increasing power to 380 KTS. At this point the front cockpit motioned a return, so I levelled off and said, "Do you want to return? Give me a thumb." Which he did.

Our circuit was something a transport aircraft fully loaded would execute, and to my surprise our gear came down on this vast circuit. Our radiator temperature climbed, and power of course was necessary. Here we sat, at least two miles on a long base leg, temp in the red, and me reluctant to change the approach as I knew how triggered up things were in the front cockpit. Our rad popped off at one mile finally, but I dared not say anything. My concern here was to try and talk as though it were a beautiful circuit. The landing roll concerned me, as he had the only brake control. I again set my feet, helped him in his pump handling, jack rabbit approach to settle him down. The landing from then on was without incident.

Never in all of my years have I had such a ride in a Spitfire. Once on the ground he talked a fantastic flight, no mention of the control or trim panic, nothing other than to say it flies beautifully. No other manoeuvers than those mentioned were flown. The exaggeration and confidence once on the ground is in keeping with the U.S.A. approach to Bullshit, and certainly not as I had been taught in the truthful, reserved fashion of the RAF.

We used to do airshows. I'd be sitting in the back doing the aerobatics, and when we landed, he'd get out take the bows and I'd walk away. And people would say, you're pretty lucky, a lousy engineer to be allowed to ride in the back.

He killed himself in a Mustang in 1975. It was just a matter of time as far as I was concerned.

Whoever said it was correct when he assessed the several millionaires who have purchased World War II aircraft to capture the excitement, glory and recognition of that era, that they are none other than extremely frustrated, untrained pilots, trying to buy that atmosphere only to find that without their obvious finesse, they emit telltale signs of disdain, an emotion involving both anger and disgust. To erase this obvious sign, they then are prone to purchase expensive, gaudy, multi-crested flying apparel, trying to give a groundborne impression as an accepted Ace of Aces. They will even go so far as to purchase a gaudy aircraft that bears the clear inscription of "Aerobatic."

From 1972 to the end of 1976, several millionaires purchased these aircraft, and in 1974-76, most of them had killed themselves in accidents involving basic fundamentals of flying. The remaining few have shied (LMF) from flying the aircraft and in one case, closed the hangar doors to let these beautiful aircraft stand collecting dust, getting flat tires and a general appearance of junk.

There were so many exceptional, brilliant aces still around at the time who would have given anything to fly those machines, but their quiet, reserved way would not allow this desire to be fulfilled, and the obvious would happen, millionaire and airplane would go straight in.

The FAA had even launched a campaign in 1976 to control this wild, erratic approach to the unqualified glamour-seeking characters who had the money but not the skill, and insisted on stringent rules for flying these masterpieces.

The airplane has no heart. You can put a hundred dollar bill on the dash; it doesn't care. It will kill a millionaire same as anyone else if you don't respect it.

The same holds for "weather flying." Some pilots press on in spite of their level of ability, just to complete a business deal, get to a hockey game, vacation, or to meet someone. Do it if you must, but be prepared to face either:
    1. Adverse weather and your ability to cope, or
    2. A cold slab somewhere, far less cozy than the worst motel.

Generally the non-realist summarizes by saying that the airplane was surrounded and the pilot trapped in a cloud, when in fact the awful truth is that the innocent airplane with the equally innocent cloud was mixed by the pilot to concoct a potential fatal combination, and this can only be handled by a trained, practiced competent instrument pilot. There are cases where an unskilled pilot will get away with it, but this only impresses him with his own ability, and contempt moves in, with the same end results.

I have personally watched this develop throughout the many years of my flying career, and no amount of advice will be accepted once the individual has entered this state of mind. What a hell of a way to go.

I started to fly the MK IX Spitfire serial MK923 about 20 years ago.

I was asked by Bill Ross, a millionaire who lived in Chicago, if I was interested in flying a Spitfire from California to Chicago. Of course. The owner was again another millionaire who had not been checked out in this aircraft. He was having great problems as the engineers on the west coast were charging him wild costs to keep the Spit serviceable.

Bill Ross knew me through the airshows in which I'd flown the dual Spit. He himself owed a P38 Lightning which he flew quite ably at the air shows. He had owned and flown numerous World War II aircraft, and was one of the few left who could speak with experience on any of them. Bill Ross said that he could re-do the Spitfire. And that's where I come into the thing, to bring it back.

Leaving Windsor found me with about $120 U.S. funds and an Esso credit card belonging to another millionaire. On arrival in Los Angeles (Oxmard) I found an engineer, Dip Davis, beneath the Spit trying to safety the controls. When I told him of my financial state he said, "Boy, we are rich. I have 10 cents that I use for collect calls, then retrieve my dime." But he said our rooms were paid for and we would use my funds for meals, room, etc, en route, and the credit card for fuel.

As I had no navigation on board except dead reckoning via map reading, Dip rented another aircraft (Mooney) to herd me to Chicago. A good move.

On landing at Palm Springs, California, the Spit boiled over. No glycol was available, so distilled water was the order of the day. Now, in order to save money, we agreed to carry the water instead of taking a taxi from the drug store to the Palm Springs airport, about two miles away in 110 degree weather. To carry the gallon jugs we tied them together and threw them over our shoulders as a coolie would. Upon arrival at the airport in this fashion, people at the airport asked, "Why not take a taxi?"

Our reply, "No bloody funds."

Blythe, on the desert, I found to be even hotter. I glided in for a landing. On take off I used the taxi strip to cut down ground time. But the canopy became unlatched on one side, and I was obliged to hold one side throughout the next leg of the trip to Deer Valley, Arizona. Christ, what next?

From Deer Valley I headed east to Winslow, over the Grand Canyon area. About half way and flying at about 9000 feet to clear the mountainous area, my fuel pressure warning illuminated. I called Dip and give him my problem. The chute available to me had not been packed or opened for over 20 years. This is what I had as an emergency route. Of course I was not about to think of baling out if the engine failed because of fuel starvation or my present problem of the fuel starvation warning. I pumped the hand emergency fuel pump until I could not longer cope and simply stopped pumping to wait for the engine to fail. To my relief the engine purred on, and I assessed the problem, as did Dip, to be a sticky pressure switch, possibility not working because of its longer period of inactivity. I landed at Winslow, content to press on without the old ring twitch as the fuel flow was correct and working properly.

From Winslow to Chicago proved to be a good run-in for the engine and without incident. I had "NO" undercarriage warning "Down" indication so Dip would land first then I would approach and he would give me the old thumbs up as I passed the touchdown point. Each aerodrome queried this operation which actually is foolproof and reminded me of the wartime procedure of a lorry for this purpose stationed on the approach end of your landing path. This procedure saved a few Spits, especially after air battle with battle damage.

At Ottumwa, Illinois the press was most interested and I flew a short acrobatic sequence for them.

Arrival at Chicago was without incident. I left the Spit in the hangar at Dupage, Illinois, the home of Ross and his P38 Lightning. Much retrofit was carried out at Dupage. A zero-rated Merlin 76 was installed (formerly the port engine from a Mosquito), and the next year I flew the Spit to Wellsville, New York for the camouflage paint scheme, using alumnagrip paint and the Spitfire re-acquired her original squadron letter 5J-Z.

Some two weeks passed and I arrived at Wellsville to fly it to Reading, West Virginia, where it won first prize as the best War Bird. I then flew to Hamilton, Ontario where it took another first prize.

I'd flown the thing for about six months before I'd even talked to its owner, Cliff Robertson.

Cliff is an extremely honest man. My association or agreement with him is that I'll display the aircraft as living history to the public if he'll keep it going.

When I met him, looking him straight in the eye, I said, "Cliff, if you think at any time that I am in your pocket, just indicate, and I'm long gone." I have *never* had any question of the charges I submit.

This particular Spit is a MK IX, serial MK923. It was built in 1944 at Castle Bromwich and flew air cover for the Normandy Invasion with #126 Squadron. In 1961 it appeared in the film "The Longest Day" filmed in France, which is where Cliff made its acquaintance. The Spit went up for sale and he bought it. He brought it back in a Flying Tiger to California. He is not checked out in the Spit. He understands the power and the problems of a high performance aircraft. He's flown a Mustang, but not a Spit.

This Spitfire was in the war. It shot down aircraft. Cliff wants young people to see what it was all about, and to see an aircraft that helped liberate the continent.

In 1986, after an engine problem, the Experimental Aircraft Association at Oshkosh were trying to get the Spit put in the museum on static display. Cliff

123 / Chapter 12

wanted it flown. He moved it to Kalamazoo Air Zoo, which is a flying museum, and unless the insurance situation puts a stop to it, all the aircraft there fly. Spitfire spends the winter in Kalamazoo. In summer, Windsor is its base between air shows.

I wouldn't give 20 minutes flying aerobatics in a Spit for 10,000 hours flying an airliner. They don't do any turns. When you're flying a Spit — when *I'm* flying it — it's right to the maximum all the time. That's flying.

Enjoying the Spitfire and Cliff's great outlook has enabled others to enjoy this great aircraft. I firmly believe the youth of today should have knowledge of how the Krauts and the Eyties were beaten. Flying the Spit today for me is living history.

A Plaque marking D DAY B4 Landing Strip Bayeux, France

124 / A Knave Among Knights in their Spitfires

Spitfire landing fees charged at Airforce Base Trenton, ON. 1982

August 20, 1985

Mr. Jerry Billing,
R. 2, South Woodslee,
Ontario.
N0R 1V0

Dear Jerry:

What a beautiful picture of you taxing in Cliff Robertson's Spitfire! – many thanks Jerry, it is nice to see that you are still thrilling the audiences at airshows and demonstrating the grace and beauty of the Spitfire wherever you go.

From time to time we hear of your demonstrations in the Spitfire and it is always from people who are clearly very impressed with what they saw. It is understandable that Her Majesty the Queen was thrilled with your show – who would not be?

Thanks again.

Sincerely Yours,

R.W. Bradford,
Associate Director

RWB/lv

Jerry was in Ottawa for the opening of the New Museum - " With the Spitfire "
BUT NOT ALLOWED TO FLY.
The person selecting the planes to fly; "Didn't like airplanes".??

125 / Chapter 12

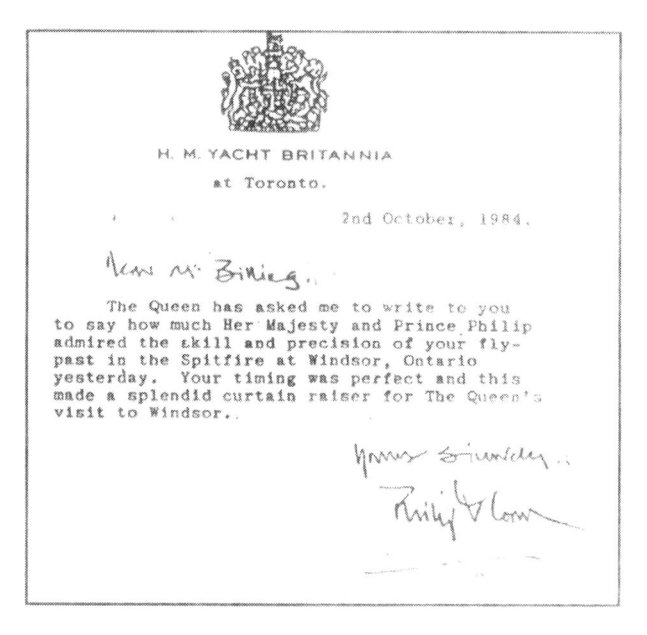

> H. M. YACHT BRITANNIA
> at Toronto.
>
> 2nd October, 1984.
>
> Dear Mr Billing,
>
> The Queen has asked me to write to you to say how much Her Majesty and Prince Philip admired the skill and precision of your fly-past in the Spitfire at Windsor, Ontario yesterday. Your timing was perfect and this made a splendid curtain raiser for The Queen's visit to Windsor.
>
> Yours sincerely,
>
> Philip V Cow

Appreciation from Her Majesty and Prince Philip on the Windsor, ON. Fly-past, 1984

Jerry in the Spitfire Mk. IV during the Fly-past.

Jerry Billing with Cliff Robertson's Spitfire Mk. IX at Octoberfest 1985

127 / Chapter 12

Jerry with Cliff Robertson's Mark IX Spitfire

Jerry in the cockpit of Cliff Robertson's Mark IX Spitfire

128 / A Knave Among Knights in their Spitfires

Mac & Dr. Peterson, Jerry & Karen, Cliff Robertson, Sue Parish, Eric Billing
Kalamazoo Air Museum, 1989.

Jerry " Low Flying " Cliff Robertson's Mk. IX Spitfire, (Jerry inset).

129 / Chapter 12

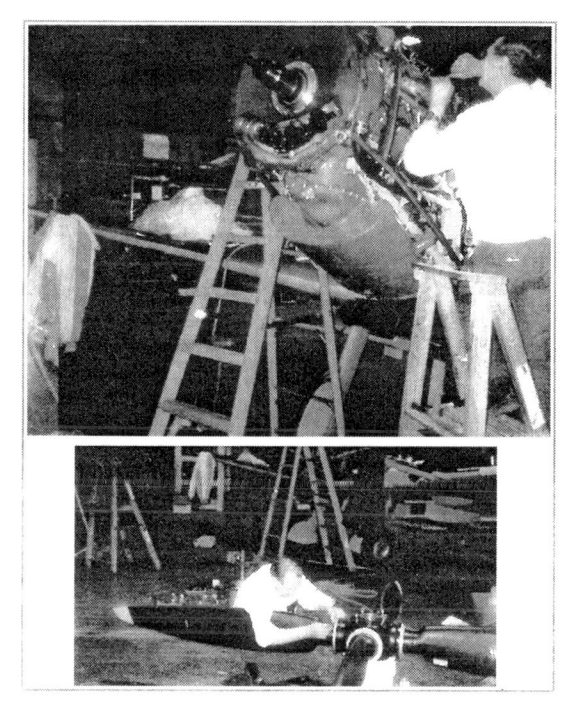

Leo Rivait fixing the Mk. IV Spitfire at Kalamazoo, Michigan, 1995

1991 Dr. Peterson - Jerry - Cliff Robertson - Eric Billing

13. FIFTY YEARS AFTER

Many years have passed since the fudge brains in the corridors of power passed rules dealing with age and pensions, but I have been able to continue. Who would have thought I'd be around after 1942?

I'm current. I still have my low-level acrobatic rating. My medical is still A-1, my eyesight 20/20.

I just had my medical and read the chart. They said, "You memorized the chart."

I said, "Put another bloody chart up."

They said, "Can you read these?"

"These" were paragraphs that get smaller and smaller. I had no trouble at all. I still don't have any trouble. I remember my uncle and my grandfather at 90 years old could read a letter without hesitation. I think that probably helped me throughout the war, the eyesight.

Since I was shot down by flak in July 1944, I have had close association with the French folks of the towns of Tribehou and Bréhal. I have returned to France several times since the war. My reception is always warm and enthusiastic. On one visit to the village of Tribehou I discovered that a wheel from the Spitfire I had crashed into the French fields had become part of a wheelbarrow, the original air still in the tire. Later, in Canada at an airshow, I told this story to another pilot, a Wardair captain. Wardair gave me two tickets to France so that the villagers of Tribehou could present me with the wheelbarrow. I, my wife, and wheelbarrow flew back to Canada courtesy of Wardair.

The French government made me an honorary citizen in 1988. In 1992 the town of Bréhal gave me a medal for "D Day" flying; for killing a Kraut, with my knife, who was trying to take me prisoner; and for the sabotage work I did while evading, in and around Bréhal. The mayor, a man, even kissed me. Christ.

My French friends have come to Canada on more than one occasion to visit my home.

C.B.C. Canada did a half hour biography on my life which is rather quite good, though little mention of Malta. A four-episode series of my personal biography also aired on television, besides many shorts.

My flight gear from Malta — my helmet and Mae West from the last time that I was shot down in Malta March 1943 — was sent to that museum about twelve years ago.

I do not, however, appreciate request for pieces of my gear from private collectors and so-called historians. For years I have been plagued with these sort of request for flying gear, log books, photographs, badges, wings, etc. What absolute nerve to ask one for his personal valuable items. We have a name for this type of person. Reminds one of the World Food Organizations begging for money and using photos of babies starving. This type of person uses the guise of history and commemoration of those unlucky types who were wounded or killed. Whit a bloody crutch, when they in the long run use it for their own monetary gain and really could not care less about the dead or they would not use this ploy. It's sick. "Be off"!!

Neither do I have any respect for those who come up to me and the Spitfire at airshows with the same questions, "How old are you?" and "How much does it cost?"

In April 1992 I passed the mark of 50 consecutive years flying Spitfires. I was surprised with a dinner in my honour with many of my old friends attending. Letters of congratulations came from the Spitfire Society, the Canadian Fighter Pilot's Association, and the Queen. The following was sent to be read at the dinner:

From: NDHQ Ottawa/Vice Chief of the Defence Staff
To: RCAF Association, Windsor

For readout at dinner in honour of Jerry Billing:

1. Jerry, it is most appropriate that your many friends and colleagues gather in Windsor tonight to pay tribute to you as you commemorate 50 consecutive years of flying the Spitfire.

2. To say that your accomplishment is an exceptional and monumental one would be an understatement. Perhaps I can resort to the vernacular of today's youth and use their favourite but most appropriate adjective AWESOME.

3. Surely your achievement must be a contender for the Guinness Book of Records. To fly for 50 years is incredible; to fly the Spitfire for 50 years is — here's that word again - awesome. I am also advised that you still have 20/20 vision and are qualified (and I assume authorized) to fly low level aerobatics. As one who has just turned 50, is writing this message looking through reading glasses and whose only flying is a mahogany bomber in the Headquarters you can only guess how envious and jealous I am.

4. If you will permit one serious note, and, as a former Commander of the Air Force, I can tell you Jerry that your wartime exploits are known to us all and serve, as do the skill and courage of your W.W. II colleagues, as a continuing source of pride and inspiration to us all. Your continuing excellence in the air at the shows you fly each year are cause for similar pride and admiration and bring great credit to yourself, the RCAF, Canada and, of course, to a truly classic fighter, the Spitfire.

5. Although many are with you tonight in Windsor, you may be assured there are thousands of others who cannot be there in person, but whose lives you have touched, directly or indirectly, who are with you in spirit.

6. I look forward to seeing you this summer on the airshow circuit. I'll be the fifty year old, wearing glasses and a 401 Squadron ball cap, drooling slightly at the sight of your beautiful airplane.

7. Have a great evening Jerry and may God bless you.

8. Lieutenant-General Fred Sutherland sends regards.

The Chairman of the Spitfire Society informs me he is, in fact, submitting my record to the Guinness Book of records.

In 1993, for another 50-year anniversary, I received the Malta George Cross 50th Anniversary Medal. This new medal was to recognize those who have survived that battle of 50 years ago.

My airshow schedule prevented me for accepting the medal in person, though British Airways offered me a flight to Malta. My request to the Canadian Defense Department for the same had been denied.

While visiting France in October 1993, I passed through Bayeau, France to visit that great museum. The curator, Dr. J.P. Benamou, recognized me from my picture in a recent magazine, approached me with the thought of my flying over the "D-Day" 50th anniversary, which he thought would be a terrific story. He tried to find a Spitfire without success — after all, who would allow some unknown to fly their aircraft?

In 1994 the French government faxed the Canadian government for the name of a Spitfire pilot who had been shot down, escaped, and still had contact with the French folk as a candidate to be honoured by the French government at events commemorating the 50th anniversary of their liberation. The RCAF proposed me, and so I was able to attend the ceremonies as a guest of the French government.

My wife and I arrived in Normandy on the 30th of May 1994. The reception was beyond belief. Twenty-six mayors of all the towns and villages in this Normandy Manche region gathered together and drew up a programme for us to visit their towns and villages and to be introduced to the people and their children, to acquaint them with the happenings of June 6, 1944. We could not possibly accept the numerous invitations to their homes. Each day, the celebration revealed a large meal with all the rich food of Normandy. The Canadian flag flew from all houses and businesses (outdoing the Yankee flag), a warm tribute by everyone. Many, many gave me thanks for leaving the security of Canada to engage the Kraut and help liberate their country from what they called the "Black Horde."

We stayed with Andre, the son of the folk who aided me. Himself in the merchant marine, Andre had been torpedoed twice and had to swim for his survival. It was his mother who bathed my blistered and bleeding feet for days, apologies flowing from her lips that I should be hurt in such a way only to help free her area. A real down-to-earth farm lady.

A red Citroen car was placed at our disposal for our entire visit. A river boat ride with several mayors was organized for us to travel along the great river La Rance in St. Malo with another great reception for a boat ride through the Carentan marshes where I crashed and survived the three and a half days in no man's land.

When asked what I would like to do on the 6th of June, I replied, "To be with the French folk and all who helped me, not to be with the draft dodger Clinton on the beachhead taking the bows."

This to them was most rewarding and surprised all of the 26 mayors at a meeting at 23:30 hours on the 31st of May. This meeting went on into the night to about 01:30 hours.

My reception in France far outweighs that given on my return to Essex after my escape and evasion. The POW's were given a large rally on the local fire engine, sirens howling, compared to my silent return with the outlook that here was a real squirrel, a civilian person. I couldn't even locate employment, for as a fighter pilot I was not wanted in the RCAF!

133 / Chapter 13

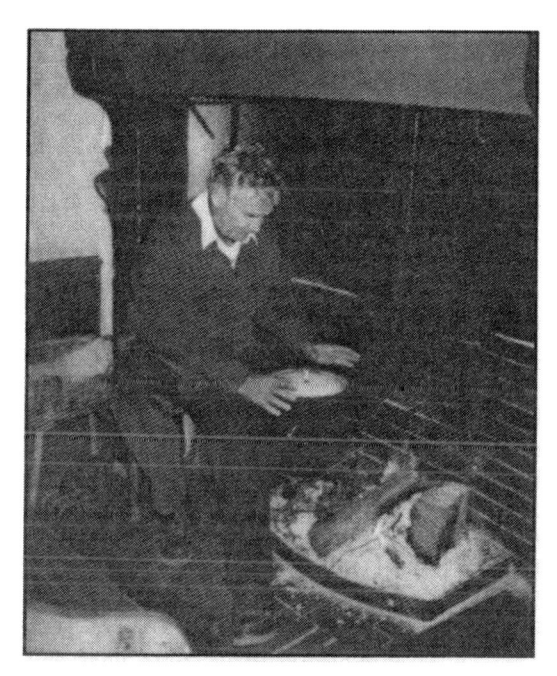

Sitting by the fire in Tribettou, France 1994. The cartridges from my Spitfire are on the " Mantle ' from when I was shot down on July 1st. 1944.

Jerry re-visiting Caen, France, (Normandy), 1994

Unfortunately the whole "D-Day" bows were taken by non-combatant politicians such as Clinton, President of the U.S.A. who evaded the Vietnam war and was primary host, mainly because of the U.S. currency spent to build that historical moment for the U.S.A. Other countries simply do not have the money for that sort of propaganda. All the flags were of moderate size except the Yankee's, which as usual were overblown. It's sad.

For the mock invasion of "D-Day", the heads of state, the British Queen, Clinton, etc. were seated in front to watch. Immediately behind them were seats reserved for a great many "D-Day" veterans. But when the ceremonies actually took place, the seats for the veterans were empty because the route to the area was cleared for only the V.I.P.s. The veterans' buses were not allowed to proceed. Even the French people could not get to work that day (a typical Yankee controlled problem) from Utah Beach to St. Mere Eglise.

Utah beach has a plaque commemorating 800 Danish sailors who lost their lives in the "D-Day" invasion, but Denmark was not invited to the celebration, nor was Russia. Both countries were extremely upset.

Our history is written that Hitler lost mainly because he turned to the East to fight Russia. However, it is also a fact that the Allies waited deliberately to delay the opening of the second front, "D-Day" in France, in the hope that Hitler and Stalin would bleed each other white on the eastern front. This then would allow the Allies and the U.S.A. to have full mastery of Europe with the minimum of casualties. Russia lost over 250,000 troops compared to the Allies' thousands. The facts are given to us in a distorted manner. (The usual propaganda).

And on the subject of propaganda, during our visit all of the French folks in Normandy told us they do not want any part in the breakup of Canada that some people of Quebec, such as Lucien Bouchard, preach. Here he is going around the country making speeches and advocating the break-up of this nation which so many people sacrificed to preserve. The French, so far from supporting such a notion, believe it ridiculous and say, "Get rid of that traitor."

135 / Chapter 13

One of my main wheels off my Spitfire that I crashed in " No Mans Land ", July 1st. 1944
Once again mounted on Cliff Robertson's Spitfire 50 years later.

Jerry reading the letter from the " Queen ", congratulating him on flying Spitfires for over 50 years. Shown here with Kyle and Bricki

14. MY AIRSTRIP

At present I am situated just outside of Essex, Ontario, where I have a small grass airstrip and hangar with a 65 horsepower Aeronca allowing me to enjoy flying most any time I wish. Quite often at daybreak I am able to get air under my arse and will take off in my pyjamas and slippers to hit the blue, enjoy the air aloft and leave the troubles of the world below.

Decon Damm, an artist from the town of Essex painted a sign for me if I would display it. It reads "Squire Billing" and hangs from my hangar. Deacon says that he has been painting for years and, not being recognized or holding a degree, he has painted on his van. "Ph.D. Doctor of Dobology". His brothers, Merly and Ross, have on their van "Damm the Painter". Characters all.

Most of my flying thrills are from the airshows today where I am able to perform in the Decathlon aircraft with the most exciting manoeuvre being the tailslide and a low, low inverted flypast.

Bob Hoover, the Rockwell pilot, is a very good friend of mine and is one who can demonstrate any type of aerobatics inside the aircraft. I really do not hold much stock in acrobatic competitions where pilots are assessed by the judges sitting in armchairs in the sun, on the ground. How can they possibly know where the ball is or recognize perfection of flying, unless they are in the bloody machine? It is dangerous to grade a man and give him a first prize when his flying is not perfect. He then only thinks he's perfect and invariably kills himself by some misuse of controls in some manoeuvre. Bob Hoover still flies in Australia and Europe, but not in the U.S. because of an argument with the F.A.A.

My father died in 1973 with a resentment towards uniforms and Europe in general. A few months prior to his death I was in his home, discussing an intended visit to Europe and how nice it was going to be to see the places again, whereupon for no reason he growled, "Why the hell don't you go and don't come back."

To say this set me back is an understatement. And as I left the room, he continued, "I've always wanted to tell him that. Now it's done."

I never saw him in his home again, and indeed I made it a point to refrain from any further communication with him. He died while I was doing an airshow in a Spitfire at Willow Run in Detroit. Following the airshow I was advised and I took the Spitfire and did one long sweep as a salute over his home and that was that.

Throughout my entire service career I assigned a portion of my pay to him, merely as a token recognition for his patience with me prior to the war. But his attitude and general hatred for uniforms always baffled me. He did not wear a uniform in World War I; this may have had some bearing on the subject.

While I was in the U.K. in 1954 - 1955 on an RAF exchange posting, I would visit Denmark frequently. In 1956 I met Karen in Canada as she had arrived from Denmark as an immigrant. We have been together since.

The sons I have are wildly blessed with their own traits. (Erik) would like to seek a flying career, while Brick realized that he must become a pilot as a passing phase. When they were about, I endeavored to fly with them daily to prepare them for their pilot's license.

137 / Chapter 14

Normandy June 1994
Top Left: Reception at Brehal
Top Right: When you have to go, you have to go.
Middle Left: How to go in France.
Middle Right: One of many dinners Celebrating 50th Anniversary.
Bottom Right: 50th Anniversary Carteville Place, Normandy

Both soloed (against all rules) when they were fifteen years old, doing loops, spins, etc. And why not, as long as I could instill in them the mandatory feeling of fear. When fear is missing and contempt moves in, one should sit on the ground until it is restored and NOT fly until it has returned. When they became of age they flew the tests and both have their pilot's license. It was quite easy, as we have the strip here and no controller to hold up flying. Simply fire up and go.

Today Brick is divorced leaving two boys in the area, Kyle and Mitch, both of whom are flying, as did Brick and Erik, before their little legs are long enough to use the rudders. (I control the rudder for them on all maneuvers). I must say it is quite impossible to keep Mitch on the ground. He is extremely keen to fly. At four years he knows the compass rose, oil temp/press and wind direction problems. He will do well.

Eric is still about, having tried a few careers, but today's Depression leaves him as I was in 1939. He thoroughly enjoys flying and has the Aeronca at his disposal at the strip.

To this day some fifty years or more on, I am still able to fly a Spitfire and to walk out my back door and fly an aircraft that I own. To be able to fly at the crack of dawn, with no one to give thumb's down because I want to be airborne, is an enormous satisfaction.

My great grandfather Major Billing led troops in the Fenian Raids era. He was rewarded by the Queen of England multi acres of land. After he became the chief magistrate, to name several villages in this area. One being North Ridge.

139 / Chapter 14

The " BILLING '" Clan

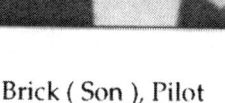

Brick (Son), Pilot   Kyle (Grandson), Training   Erik (Son), Pilot

" Mitch " - at four years of age he is aware of the four points of the compass and once airborne is never lost. He has engine temp. and pressures and is aware of wind and it's use.

One day as he was in the front seat of the 65 HP Aeronca, I took off ' downwind ', he immediately started to cry. I said " what's the problem ", He said " land ", once on the ground he said " airplane in hanger ", I shut down. He got out of the plane and with long strides went into the house and told Karen: ' " Jerry did it wrong, he took off downwind", All this and only four years old.

IN MEMORY OF

Generally, in the heat of the battle some of the chaps would be shot down (killed), their names would be mentioned for the next day or two, then, completely forgotten "forever..." To me, their names should remain a reminder, for everyone to realize their security (full bellies etc.) and to not be under the Black Horde of Nazism and Fascism. It was a great sacrifice for those who gave up their safe living at home, and volunteered to rid the world of such corruption, only to gain a hole, in either the ground or at sea.

- Essex Scottish Dieppe Raid - I
- Malta Blitz - II
- "K-France" - III
- Post-war Canada - IIII

I
Llye McKeecan
Jack Wortley
Chuck Scheoley
Lawrence Galliver
Butch Taylor
Newt Barnard
Harold Mallott

II
Sgt. George Beurling
Sgt. Lloyd Brown
Sgt. Admiral Bird
Sgt. Mike Askey

III
... Gunston
Babe Fenwick
Cummings
Stanford Tuck
Gordie Trooke
Odie Levere
Sgt. Gordie Bray
Sgt. Pete Peters
Sgt. Pete Carter
Sgt. Williams
Sgt. Red Schewell
Sgt. Carmody
Sgt. Jeff Guy
Sgt. Miller
F/O Maynard
F/L Hetherington
Sgt. Danny Hartney
Sgt. Goodyear
F/L Withy
C/O Prosser Hanks

Alex Dickie
Stan Turner
Zip Zobel
Eep Wood
Tiny Thompson
Larry Spurr
Ted Griffin
Al McLaren
Buck McNair
George Keefer
Sid Mills
Wilcox, Affleck
Mitchner
Wendy Reid
Cuth Betson Cathberts 84
Goody Goodwin
Dave Fairbanks
Ernie Glover
Lloyd Hubbard
P/O Park

141 / In Memory Of

IIII
Dennis Tatomir
Nelson Boose
Dr. Ken Foster
Dr. Anderson

John Voderk
Art Charlton
Dr. Bruner

142 / A Knave Among Knights in their Spitfires

"LEST WE FORGET"

The chief prosecutor in the trial of major German war crimes of WW II, said, ..."apologists for defeated nations are sometimes able to ply upon the sympathy and magnanimity of their victors, so that the true facts, never authoritatively recorded, become obscured and forgotten....

There have been numerous other war crimes trials the proceedings of which have been published, and, there for all to read ... but ... many have no time to do so, and many would not wish to, if they had.... "

To have many Nazi war criminals today (50 years on) living a free life in Canada, without a grain of justice towards them is beyond reasoning — why? Why??

The Italians justice for Mussolini, when they hung his mistress and him, in their public square, upside down, then drove a metal shaft down his rectum, surely must indicate that his WW II antics were not proper.

It is utterly impossible to understand how newer generations could overlook and dispel such atrocities as...

TREBLIHKA - thousands of bodies, where the Germans destroyed the camp and planted trees (3/4 of a million cremated)
LIDICE - the German massacre of the whole town...
BIRKENAU - before the crematorium was built, bodies were burnt in huge pits...
TULLE - the mass hanging of patriots...
AUSCHWITZ - Ilse Koch-Disfiguring women - using them as human guinea pigs...
BUCHENWALD - the German production of shrunken heads...
BELSEN - where British troops after "VE Day", had to clear the area of piles of dead bodies, with bulldozers (that lay about) into open mass, 50-feet-wide, deep trenches.
THE WARSAW GHETTO - this history will not and must not be forgotten. The recent bombing in Oklahoma City killing a mere 115 plus — is a mere drop in the bucket compared to the thousands and thousands of Warsaw Ghetto killed.

A WAR TO END ALL WARS
"What *utter nonsense*,
it will *never* happen..."

The deep-rooted hatred between Christians and Moslems gave way to the Great Christian-Moslem War in the 13th century, which "Still goes on"... The Christians were badly beaten by the Moslems. "Whose side is the almighty on?"... If it exists!!!!....

COMMENTS

Whether one wants to believe it or not, it is a fact, that pilots on operation Squadrons in 1940 were of a select few and in 1944 one had to be one of the group, or, you just never got a squadron. A real closed shop and "Buddy, Buddy deals". Many capable pilots sat out the war, or, flew other types as they had no contact to join Spitfire Squadrons.

Dick Audet: Was shot down strafing a train, killed. Spent most of the war in Canada. Training.

Russ Bannock: Mosquito pilot, set himself up in later years to become head of DeHavilland, Toronto when I was test pilot there. A gripey type that I really didn't appreciate.

George Beurling: I first ran into him in UK early 1942, flew with him in Malta and was in Malta when he was shot down on this last sortie Malta 1942. In 1944 I again flew with him out of Biggin Hill UK. He wanted to get a section of four Mustangs (lots of fuel big range) and fly as a foursome deep into enemy country to pick off training schools. I was to be one of the four, however, the wheels thought this to be not cricket and distasteful? That was that. In early 1948 he left to go to Israel, but his Norseman was sabotaged by Eyties and he was killed.

Lloyd Vernon Chadburn: In 1944 he was at Tanegmere on 127 wing, I was on 126 wing. He was on a sweep over France when on a 180-degree turn his #2 ran into him killing both. Destroyed 6.6.

Charles: A real miserable type (good, excellent pilot), but I never appreciated him although he treated me very well, even went so far as to ensure that I got back into the RCAF 1948, so? Destroyed 15.5.

Stocky Edwards: A real fine quiet guy, too quiet almost, never got too far in rank, no education. He did get the bar and DFM, rare prizes for non-commissioned pilots. Embarrassing for the King to hand out, as officers generally are par excel. for awards. D-13.

Dave 'Foo' Fairbanks: He flew Tempests mostly. I met him in 1966 when I joined DeHavilland as test pilot in Toronto. We went to Vietnam twice 1967 1968. We also did airshows together in France, UK, Germany, Sweden, Belgium, and many other. Bloody heart gave out in 1978 in Toronto. (Brick has his watch presently).

George Ungart Hill: Good type, flew very little with him. He was on other squadrons. Car accident got him. Destroyed 11.

Bert Houle: Again this guy I knew well, but was on other squadrons. Destroyed 8.

George Keefer: Quiet guy, flew with him many times. Was our wing/Comdr.. We were on either side of Norm Fowlow over France when in one second he was flying there and in the next instant he was blown to hell before our eyes, a fantastic sight to see, but rather rough on old Norm. Keefer gave me good head and allowed me to do and fly as I wished, and, I did. He is director of Canadair and often asked me to fly test pilot there, but Montreal you know, too many Zombies. (Good solo trips to France from Biggin Hill 1944). Destroyed 12.

'Hap' Ian Farmer Kennedy: A very close friend I have known since Malta 1942. He was beside me when last I was shot down by flak, July 1, 1944, crashing in "No-mans land". Hap often assured me that he was so upset about me crashing that if I had not exited from the smashed Spit that he was determined to crash land beside my aircraft and help me out. Hap was so dedicated and detested the enemy so much that I have seen him drop to his knees (when one of our guys was chasing an ME 109 across our drome in France) crying, "Get that bastard, Christ, get that son of a bitch, Kill him." Once Hap got into position for the kill, no one got away. He loved it and why not. Destroyed 12.

Johnny Kent: A real distinct killer who ensured no gone got away alive, regardless. An older chap who could not stand anyone making an error. When two pilots were killed and mangled he had the bodies laid on two wood boards, then put them on display on the parade grounds, and had all the pilots march by, stop, and take the sight in, saying, "Now you bastards that's what you will get for low flying." But I really must say it did little for me as I was of the opinion that low flying done properly can be a lifesaver. Kent was in trouble for that action. Destroyed 13.

Kipp: A twin night fighter pilot who was killed trying a low roll in a Vampire jet, completely out of his environment, but he had the rank and who is to say no?

Grissle Klersey: A real Harpo Marx type, baggy pants, curly unkept hair, pockets in tunic torn and generally sloppy. He was a sprong pilot on 401 in '44 when I knew him, but became quite deadly in the latter stages of the war in Europe. He was killed flying back to UK, was in weather and let down into a hard-centered cloud. Destroyed 14.

Don (Laubhead) Laubman: I flew with him on several occasions. He too excelled later in the war. In 1952 he was leader of RCAF 1st Vampire Aerobatic Team which I was part of. I real grumpy type. Destroyed 15.

John McElroy: Malta type 42. He was on the same squadron as Beurling. In 1952, I had him as student getting him his introduction category. He later came to jet F86 OTU where I checked him out and prepared him for a squadron in Germany. Destroyed 14.

John McKay: Didn't drink or smoke. Lived only to fly, a real recluse, but a loyal type. Destroyed 11.

Wally McLeod: Again I knew him well, but he was on another squadron. Destroyed 21.

Buck Robert Wendell McNair: Great guy and because of him and Lorne Cameron I could be assured of joining a squadron at any time. When I returned to UK 1944 after one month in Canada I rebelled at all orders, told them to shove it and took the train to Biggin Hill. Buck on my arrival said, "Well done, Jerry, to hell with HQ. I'll call them and fix it up. Good Hunting." Buck always told me, "Jerry, if you want to get ahead in this Airforce, take your chute out to the airplane, drop it on the ground, shit on the tail and go back to your desk. The wheels hate airplanes and are not impressed with those who fly them." Buck died of Leukemia caused by the hurts of the many times he was shot down, burnt, broken-up and hurting for many years. He suffered quietly without too much complaint. I saw him a few months prior to his death. He said, "It's been too short, Jerry, but Christ the pain sometimes is rough, too bad we cannot handle it like years ago." Destroyed 15.

Mitch Mitchner: I knew him very well, but again he was on another squadron. This does not mean we weren't in the same sky together, only once on the ground each went his way etc. Died of Leukemia in Ottawa 1974. Destroyed 10.

'Rod' Long John Smith: Malta type, brainy guy who could really fly. After the war he completed degrees as a lawyer, engineer, as bad as old Hap. real perfectionist, had 6 kills in Malta, but joining 127 (W) back in UK the feeling Malta types stopped his promotion until later. Destroyed 13.2.

Marble-eyes Stan Turner: A much older type who we all looked up to as a father. He always allowed me to do just as I wished and even though I used to beat up the station unmercifully he never once mentioned or noted it, but told everyone he can do as he wishes, I'll never question him. He was a good type. A Battle of Britain Ace. Destroyed 14.

W/C Prosser Hands DSO DEC/Bar: Malta Co 1942. He had a special Spit lacking the carb panel (for desert), would not allow anyone to fly his aircraft, but he ensured I got a crown F/Sgt. and told the chief if I wanted to I could fly his aircraft (P.P.H.) I had continued contact with him when I was at AFDS in UK. He was day F/Ldr CO. Prosser was #2 prior to war doing Aeroes (Siskins) with wings tied by ribbons. He died 1993 in South Africa (heart). Destroyed 14.

W/C Bob Braham: DSO/bar DFC/2 bars: Night fighter RAF joined RCAF in 1954 went to HQ for interview (promotion) was told you do not have sufficient education, he replied, "Hitler never asked for my education qualifications." He was really upset. Died of Cancer 1978. Destroyed 29.

Capt. Rene Royer: Free French. I was with Rene on the many, many Rhubarbs we flew from 19 Squadron Perranport 1942 Cornwall. We ran into FW 190's off Cherbourg on a couple of occasions. The first E A I saw. Rene lasted until 1944. Killed in action. Destroyed 5.

Lt. Emile LeBlanc: Free French on 19 Squadron Perranport 1942. Emile was lost, killed in action 1942. Destroyed 5.

F/S/FO Red (Scarlet) Schewell: From Owen Sound of 249 Squadron Malta 1942. Scarlet was on the same initial training as I and arrived in the UK on the same bloody boat. He had many dogfights at Malta with several kills, but like everyone else no witness. As Sgt.'s our main desire was to get the distinguished flying medal (a rare achievement) but he was never awarded anything. A terrific Spit pilot. He was killed in 1943 back in the UK. Destroyed 6.

Some of the other chaps I knew, but had little nor not association with. Many comments and episodes are not included simply because there are so many that one is not reminded of until something or a happening brings to memory those terrific days.

147 / Comments

Prior to Jerry's last Spitfire flight at the 1994 airshow. Jerry at the age of 73.

FINAL WORDS

I must express in sincere appreciation for the great loyalty and understanding give to me (an extremely rare occurrence) by the following:

Movie actor (Academy-Award Winner) Mr. Cliff Robertson. As honest a person to walk the soil..."anywhere"!

The Canadian Fighter Pilots Association. A group of chaps who would take flak to save one's life, and did.

The Spitfire Society in the U.K. What a magnificent society to be associated with.

To all who assisted me during my Spitfire acrobatic shows. I was most strict with the Spitfire and at times demanded that gloves be worn to handle the magnificent bird (after all) the fuselage resembles a woman's leg ... and I was in it for over 52 1/2 years.

Alex Hewshaw and Laddie Lucas — true Brits to the end..."Don't let Europe rule Britannia"!!!

To the people of France — who put their head on the block to save mine...

I have heard of a pilot crashing and being killed in an aircraft, many people remark: "That is the way he would have liked to go." What an absolutely horrible way to die.
As Alex Hensahw (a very close friend and exceptional pilot who test flew most of the Spitfires of W.W. II and was responsible for perfecting that great aircraft) says, "We shall fall from our perch one day."
When my fall occurs I should like to go as my grandfather did — the night before he died, he had a death grip on a nurse, saying, "Just one more." He was 'never' given 'his' last rites.

I could *never* get people in the Air Force to understand that I joined the force as a pilot — to fly — not as a *clerk*. As they always insisted. This I fought for to the end.

149 / Final Words

ADDRESS REPLY TO:
THE SECRETARY,
DEPARTMENT OF NATIONAL DEFENCE FOR AIR,
OTTAWA, ONTARIO.

OUR FILE C.-J.18371 (DPC/OC3)
REF. YOUR
DATED

ROYAL CANADIAN AIR FORCE

OTTAWA, 18th January, 1945

CONFIDENTIAL

Flying Officer G. D. Billing,
Essex, Ontario.

Dear Flying Officer Billing:

It is regretted that cancellation of your release from the R.C.A.F. cannot be effected at this late date.

There is no urgent demand for pilots in transport work, nor does your flying experience make you especially suited for such employment, since you were a fighter pilot.

Yours sincerely,

(J. A. Easton)
Group Captain,
for Chief of the Air Staff.

Handwritten note:

NOTE

NO-ONE LISTENING
I WAS PUT ON A SPECIAL CLASS "E" RESERVE & COULD BE RECALLED — I REMAINED ON THIS UNTIL "V E" DAY ALL PENSIONABLE TIME --- BUT NOT PAID ?!?

SOUNDS

Sunbeams
Glint from his goggles
As the pilot, humbled
In his open cockpit, his
White plume applauding
The propwash cadenzas,
Waves farewell
To his adversary.
Spinning and burning,
Gentlemen weaving their art
In sky play
With spider threads.
Grateful for the battle
That each must lose –
But the game-plan, you know,
One-on-one:
As it was for Cain and Abel and
Saracen and crusader.
A life, birth, death and
Everything between
Reduced to a moment's silence
As victor transmutes to vanquished,
Toasting
At the officers' mess that evening,
The fire-bird's final plunge.
The craggy talons, scorched
Crumpled wings
Will hunt no more
Or be hunted.

Today, gentlemen kill
Differently, with indifference.
Computer consoles, sonar, radar,
Minute-man missiles
Give the planet just seconds
To survive.
White ignition clouds
Slap the tail, and
The Sparrow leaps
From its swept-wing pod,
Sent on its mission by
An unwaving unhelmeted
Miniscule electron.
A death's watch vigil is
Kept in the muted dark-room red,
Waiting for the electron's wink
Confiding that
The target is destroyed
A universe away.

Echoes of a
Tolling bell
Pirouette from star
To star
And nova-like
Spin away to
Meet at the beginning
And the end

And none are left
To listen

Just sounds

G. I. BERNSTEIN,
220 Tecumseh Road, West,
WINDSOR, Ontario. N8X 1G1

For those who do know & are especially grateful, are my brother & myself who wouldn't be around, without those gallant knights in their Spits.

AD ASTRA.

George Bernstein. M.D.

151 / Final Words

AMBASSADE DE FRANCE
AU CANADA

Ottawa, 25 May 1995

Dear Sir,

I am pleased and honoured to inform you that by decree on 3 April 1995, the President of the Republic of France appointed you *Chevalier dans l'Ordre National du Mérite*. This honour is being bestowed on you as part of the 50th anniversary of the cessation of hostilities in the Second World War in Europe.

By granting you this pretigious title, the authorities of my country wish to honour your distinguished and courageous contribution to the liberation of France.

It would give me great pleasure to present you with this decoration at the French Ambassador's Residence in Ottawa on 14 July 1995 at the reception I traditionally give to mark France's National Day. I would be very grateful if would let me know whether you can attend this event, which will be held in the late afternoon of 14 July. You may contact my staff (social secretary) by telephone at (613) 789-0960. Alternatively, if you are unable to attend, the presentation may be organized by contacting the Consul-General of France in Toronto.

Please accept my sincere congratulations.

Yours sincerely,

CHEVALIER
"KNIGHT Hoo."

A. SIEFER-GAILLARDIN

Monsieur Jerry BILLING
RR N° 2
SOUTH WOODSLEE (Ontario)
N0R 1V0

RIDEAU HALL

LA CHANCELLERIE
THE CHANCELLERY

February 16, 1996

Dear Mr. Billing:

    I am pleased to inform you that the Government of Canada, on the advice of the Honours Policy Sub-Committee, has approved the request of the Government of France to appoint you Knight of the National Order of Merit.

    As per our policy, this approval was published in the Canada Gazette six months after the donor country was informed of the decision of the Committee. A copy of the Gazette is attached as well as a guide entitled "Wearing of Orders, Decorations and Medals".

    May I take this opportunity to offer you my warmest congratulations.

Yours sincerely,

James C. Gervais
Lieutenant General (Retd)
Deputy Secretary

Enclosures

Mr. Jerry Billing
R.R. No. 2
South Woodslee, Ontario
N0R 1V0

DGD/mw

1 PROMENADE SUSSEX / 1 SUSSEX DRIVE
OTTAWA CANADA K1A 0A1

Laddie Lucas Comments   He was a C.O. at Takali, Malta in the middle of the Blitz, 1942.

He killed 18 plus of the Black Hoard and stood out as a supporter of Canadian Pilots.

My close association with him until he died a couple years ago.

When Air Marshal Keith Park met us on arrival (Off the carrier) he spoke to me, and asked what sqdn. I came from, I said #19- with Czechs and Poles- He quickly responded saying "Great, you'll do O.K.!"- then promptly climbed into a Hurricane and took off into the air raid in progress.

Laddie's comments were a hell of a great senior commander "He will fight rather than be a paper pusher so obvious" Year 2009 (Dial up www.jerrybilling.com)

I last saw Laddie in 1994, when he said to me "Christ Jerry, when are you going to hang up your helmet and gloves?" But, be careful as no one or very few appreciate what you stand for—

That shows today the government and Vet. Affairs anti vet outlook coupled with Lakeshores officials Despise with an Arrogant, supercilious aversion against me, and regard me as unworthy---

The letter to the Queen revealed immediate support for a Veteran- Rare.

A CANADIAN KNIGHT
HAS
EQUAL RIGHTS SINCE 1996

CPSIA information can be obtained at www.ICGtesting.com
Printed in the USA
LVOW10s0903160914

404170LV00001B/20/P